Ronnie Thompson is an ex-prison officer. He saw more corruption and violence in his years in the service than most people see in a lifetime. Ronnie is now a full-time writer, and also writes for film and television. He lives with his partner and their two children.

'Hard-hitting and powerful. This is one man's journey from darkness to light' John King, author of *The Football Factory* and *The Prison House*

'Ronnie's done it again – *Banged Up* is non-stop from start to finish. He really is a master of the prison genre. I can't wait to see what he does next' Garry Bushell, journalist and television presenter

'Raw, biting, and unapologetic, Ronnie Thompson is a rare talent with a uniquely authentic vision of prison life and the outlaw souls that occupy it . . . Fast, unexpected, and deadly accurate. You won't know what's hit you' Ron L. Brinkerhoff, screenwriter, *The Guardian* and *Bent*

By Ronnie Thompson and available from Headline Review

Screwed
Banged Up

BANGED UP
THE TRUTH ABOUT LIFE
AS A CRIMINAL

RONNIE THOMPSON

headline
review

First published in 2010
by HEADLINE REVIEW
An imprint of Headline Publishing Group

First published in paperback in 2010
by HEADLINE REVIEW

8

Cataloguing in Publication Data is available from the British Library

ISBN 978 0 7553 1987 9

Typeset in ZapfElliptical by Avon DataSet Ltd,
Bidford on Avon, Warwickshire

Printed and bound by CPI Group (UK) Ltd, Croydon, CR0 4YY

Headline's policy is to use papers that are natural, renewable and
recyclable products and made from wood grown in sustainable
forests. The logging and manufacturing processes are expected to
conform to the environmental regulations of the country of origin.

HEADLINE PUBLISHING GROUP
An Hachette UK Company
338 Euston Road
London NW1 3BH

www.headline.co.uk
www.hachette.co.uk

For Exile Parade, a top band, top blokes
– the next big thing

CONTENTS

Author's Note   ix

Life of Crime   1

Clint Eastwood   3

A Clockwork Gun   49

Lord, Don't Slow Me Down   67

The Filth and the Fury   77

Invaders Must Die   101

Darkly Dreaming Donnie   113

A Tale of a Chemical Romance   123

If the Devil Exists   145

The Jab, the Shield, the Visit   159

Ultraviolence (It Gets You)   179

The Shining 203

A Con formerly Known as Davey 233

Departed 255

The Colour Red (Don't Look) 275

F.E.A.R. 287

Bridge the Gap 297

A Bus Could Run You Over 303

AUTHOR'S NOTE

Everything in this book is real. The crack heads, smack heads, drug dealers, arse kickers, pimps, nonces, grasses, troublemakers, meatheads, knobheads, dickheads, scumbags, shit bags, time wasters and the toe rags exist in all prisons. The bend ups, cock ups, wrap ups, fuck ups, rub downs, strip searches, fights, barricades, riots, corruption and ineptitude are as told to me by David Sommers, an amalgamation of he cons I've spoken to over the years. All events are set in the fictitious prison, HMP Romwell. 'The Well' is not based on any individual prison. It is an amalgam created for security reasons and to allow the action to take place all under one roof. I've also become quite fond of the name.

When one is released from the prison of self, that indeed is freedom! For self is the greatest prison.

When this release takes place, one can never be imprisoned. Unless one accepts dire vicissitudes, not with dull resignation but radiant acquiescence, one cannot attain freedom.

Words attributed to 'Abdul'l-Bahá

LIFE OF CRIME

Villain. Thug. Outlaw. All labels given to those associated with crime. My name is David Sommers. I'm fifty-one years old and for the best part of my life I've been a professional criminal. Using the word professional may offend some people, but crime was my line of work and, believe me, I needed special training to be good at it. I wasn't a petty thief or anything like that. I was a high-ranking key figure in a huge network of organised crime.

You're not going to hear my tale of woe. The story of how I came from a broken family or that abuse led to my incessant life of thuggery. In fact, my father is a retired pastor and my mother was the most loving and caring person I could have wished for. I had excellent parents. My brother Adam and I were brought up in a fairly nice place. It wasn't Surrey, but it wasn't Moss Side either. Not rich, not poor – we were surviving well enough among the rest of the community. Our school wasn't bad either; it turned out some good and not-so-good results. Adam went on to be a cardiologist; I went on to be an eight-man unlock at The Well.

Prison is a career hazard when you choose a path on the wrong side of the law. Crime comes with a tax-free salary, but when you get caught, you pay with your liberty. Metaphorically speaking, I've contributed well over the forty per cent bracket, having spent nearly two decades inside. I'm not asking for sympathy. I deserved it. But did I deserve everything that's happened to me? I'll leave that for you to decide.

This is a frank account of my life of crime. But it's not an apology. I think it's important to tell it how it really was. I've had many years to come to terms with what I've done and who I was. I've been punished for what I did and when I say I repent, I mean it. Lots of people believe in karmic law. I do now.

CLINT EASTWOOD

The foul stench hit me. Right at the back of my throat. It was more like a flavour than a smell. I could actually taste it. Unwashed skin, rotting teeth and clothes that hadn't seen the inside of a washing machine for years. That mixed with a toilet that didn't flush, filled to the top with shit. That's what I woke up to, when I was banged up in cell A4-23.

I'd been awake for most of the night. I had a lot on my mind. A plan I needed to carry out. My pad mate, Terry, was a noisy bastard, as well. He suffered from nightmares, so occasionally he'd break out in sporadic screams. Sometimes I'd tolerate it; other times I'd punish him.

It was quarter to five in the morning, day hadn't even started to break and I was wide eyed, pacing up and down the cell. The biggest enemy you have inside is time. The measure of existence can crush a man. Every part of him. Grown men – hard, violent men – have been totally broken by it. They've been driven to fight like animals – kill, rob and maim. Time is the invisible enemy. It creeps up on you and leaves you and your thoughts to fight it out.

I'd been inside for nearly nine years. When I wasn't fighting, I'd found the perfect way to deal with time – crack and heroin. Crack would raise my awareness; make me focused, like an adrenaline-fuelled maniac. Heroin would cuddle me like a silk blanket, removing any worries and stress that entered my orbit. Together, they made the perfect cocktail. Deadly, but blissful for the unstable and wayward mind.

As I paced up and down the cell that morning, I didn't just hear voices but screams, ferocious and loud. I breathed heavily; I felt my chest tighten. I was only wearing my pants and vest, but they were drenched with sweat. My stubble had grown into a straggly beard. My hair was almost shoulder length and unkempt; it was greasy and damp from my leaking skin.

It was early August, in the middle of a blistering summer. It was a night where, even in a civilian bed, you'd toss and turn because of the heat. In a cell, the temperature can literally treble. During the day it's like a sauna; at night, a bird cage with a solid top and sides – zero ventilation.

I walked over to the window to try and get some air. I couldn't breathe. The window had a small pane, divided by metal bars. Outside the window, there were more bars fixed to the building, so if you did open your window, it wouldn't go further than six or seven inches. That morning, the window was already opened to its full capacity. I started to bang it against the outer bars, trying to open it further, knowing I couldn't.

'Piece. Of. Shit.' I yelled as I banged it.

Terry started to stir.

'The fuck you doing?' he said, in sleepy anger.

I moved into his personal space. 'How about I squeeze your head in the gap? That will get me some more fucking air, won't it?'

I stared him in the eyes. He knew I was off key. One more word, I would have unleashed. He put his head back on the pillow.

Pacing again, I looked at my watch. Ten to five. I couldn't take any more. I needed a clear head for the day. And a drug-free day wasn't an option. I loaded my homemade pipe to the top with crack. I wasn't quiet about it. I couldn't care less if I disturbed Terry any more than I already had. I wanted the voices to stop. The pain to go away.

I slumped on to my bed, the bottom bunk. I put my lighter to the crystals. It crackled as I inhaled. The sharp burning hit the back of my throat and I felt better right away. It had an instant psychological release. Just the thought of being filled with crack was enough to smooth the edges. Even before I felt the hit, I felt high at the thought of release.

The squeaking of Terry's bed screamed out in my head as he shuffled around. I continued to light and puff, until I'd used it all. I stood up and went to get my next comfort. Heroin. I had started to feel a little more focused.

'It's five o'clock in the fucking morning, Davey – what you playing at?'

I turned round to see a frustrated Terry sitting on the edge of his bed. I walked calmly over. 'Taking the edge off, that's all.'

'You're losing the . . .'

Before he could finish, I punched him hard in the face, knocking him back on to the bed.

'ARGH!' he screamed.

'The fuck it's got to do with you, mug?'

I hit him two or three more times. Crack cocaine and patience don't go well together. Crack and insanity is more appropriate. I was a true example of that.

'All right! Leave it out, I'm sorry.'

I let him go. I was sweating even more.

Terry sat up, wincing as he did so. He wasn't shocked. He wasn't even that scared. He was accustomed to my regular violent outbursts. He'd been a punch bag for me on more than one occasion. Because of my unpredictable nature, he could never gauge what was acceptable to me and what wasn't. Some days, I'd listen to his friendly advice, seeing him as a respected confidante; other days, he'd ask me for some ketchup and I'd smash a chair over his head. Like a victim of domestic violence, he'd kind of learned to live with it.

I folded up some tin foil, so I could chase the dragon.

'Here, have some,' I offered. It was my kind of apology. Heroin at five in the morning. What a good friend I was.

'Too early for me, mate.' Terry looked at me, then reconsidered. 'Actually, mate, I think I'll have one.'

I don't know what made him change his mind. Fear perhaps? That's the most likely reason, I guess. Even I didn't know what I was capable of. I'd hear voices and then the pipe would make them disappear. When I was on the pipe, I was capable of almost anything. Hurting or even killing anyone within my reach, if need be.

For the next few hours, Terry and I smoked a lot of heroin. I was out of my mind on drugs, but I can recall everything about that day. I was alert. I no longer felt the heat. My chest felt easier, my cage more bearable and bigger than ever.

As light began to break, I started to hear the usual shouts from window to window. Our way of communicating with each other when behind the door. During the day, the shouts were the loudest. Morning it was just one or two. The shouts were a sign that morning unlock was just around the corner.

I heard the screws on the landings doing the count. It was a familiar noise of a cell door flap opening and slamming shut. Being counted and rubbed down was no different than having a cup of tea. Not to me or most of the lads. It was a strange experience at first. You'd feel violated; having some man touch you every time you moved to a different area of the prison. That's how it was, though: just a normal part of the prison day. Part of the life. A whole, different world that exists under the noses and out of the way of society.

Terry and I hid our drug paraphernalia out of view.

The early count finished, more cons began to wake. The noise of doors being kicked and shouts of 'Guv' became clearer. Good morning, HMP Romwell.

Terry and I got out our prison tracksuits. We were supposed to have our kit changed each week, but I couldn't remember the last time I'd received one. Staffing was the problem apparently. Actually, it was the fat, lazy bastards sitting in their chairs doing nothing that was the problem. They'd made a job out of being idle. Arse and scratch was top of their agenda. Not all, perhaps, just some. The other problem was that I was usually busy fighting, sleeping or taking drugs, so when kit was actually being changed, I was too distracted by one of my more favourable pastimes.

I wanted to have a wash. The tap on the sink constantly trickled water, so pressing it down did nothing. The flow just continued at the same pace. All night long that noise echoed around the cell, adding to the torture of my surroundings. Countless times I'd asked to have it fixed. When I spoke to my personal officer, Mr Cramfield, about it, he said, 'Go fuck yourself, Sommers, I hope it drives you mental.'

I wasn't the most liked inmate, as you can imagine. I wasn't a nice man. I was disturbed. Mr Cramfield had experienced my wrath many times over the years. I'd hospitalised him, thrown shit at him and spent hours upon hours taking the piss out of him. My head and his boot had met on several occasions. He gave as good as he got, though, that's for sure. We hated each other.

The water came out of the tap at an awkward, frustrating, pain-in-the-arse speed. Fast enough to echo loud and clear round the cell, too slow for any sort of decent wash. So, I dampened my dirty skin and rubbed in some blackened, odourless soap. As usual, I couldn't rinse it off properly, so I was just adding to the grimy film of hardened soap that had built up from days of cell washing. We had set times for showers but, like with the kit change, I was always too busy with something else.

Terry had his broken wash, too, which caused us to bump into each other. Sometimes this would cause punch ups, but when we were smashed out of our brains, more often than not, it would cause a laugh.

Our door flap opened and I saw Cramfield's eye look

through. He held my stare for a few seconds longer than was necessary, so I gave him the finger.

Once we were both dressed, Terry rolled a couple of spliffs. Although I'd taken lots of drugs that morning, I still wasn't completely relaxed. As other lads began to wake, the shouts became more frequent. The sound of the screws walking around, preparing for the day, was more evident. All these noises were as familiar to me as the sound of my own voice, but my paranoia was getting bad. Extremely bad. I jumped at every shout. Each footstep sounded like an atomic bomb dropping. The tap was as noisy as Niagara Falls. Terry's small clock was driving me insane. Each time the second hand moved, it was like a shock of lightning. My chest felt looser but my breathing sounded like the base tone of a hurricane. Every damn noise smashed through my skull.

'Fucking noisy this morning, isn't it?'

Terry looked at me in confusion.

I went over to the window, to join in the shouts.

'SHUT UP, YOU MUGGY CUNTS!' I screamed.

I went over and started kicking the cell door, screaming at each bang.

'Your poxy clock is getting on my tits, an' all.'

I stamped on it until the mechanics were no longer on the inside. I pulled at my hair. The noise.

'Sit down. I'll roll another,' Terry reasoned.

The noise was too much. Too loud. Unbearable. It was

frightening and becoming almost impossible to control myself. I felt fear, like a burning fire, spreading through my whole body. As much as I tried to extinguish it, I was actually fuelling it. It was a vicious circle of self abuse.

We sat there finishing up our smokes. The screw on the ground floor shouted, 'SEND DOWN THE FOURS', letting the staff on my landing know that they were ready to receive us. Morning unlock was a controlled exercise. One landing at a time would be unlocked and sent down. It makes sense – each landing held anything up to eighty prisoners. It was for their safety and to help them keep control. The morning regime was a conveyor belt of activity: unlock, meds, exercise, association – or 'sowsh' – and workshops, food, and then bang up.

I heard the doors being cracked open on my landing. It's a loud noise. The keys are heavy, the door handles big, so when an officer unlocks your door it is loud. It got louder as they made their way across the landing, getting closer to our cell. The closer they got, the happier I became. I knew I was about to step out of my cage. It wasn't freedom, but it was as close as you can get to it inside.

It was getting louder. One door cracked open, then another. One more. It was so loud it echoed in our cell. I stood by the door, jumping up and down like Ricky Hatton before a world title fight. The anticipation. The excitement. The key went into our door. AT LAST. The handle cracked and the door opened an inch or two. By the time I'd pushed it fully open, the screw was already unlocking the next two doors along. Conveyor belt.

I stepped on to the landing, hearing the sounds of morning madness. The wing was a huge space. The Well is a Victorian prison, so it has massive residential wings that look like giant church halls, only less decorated and not so pretty. Think *Porridge* but bigger. The walls are a dirty magnolia and the doors a blinding green. The landing is about four-feet wide, with hand rails opposite the cell doors.

I leaned over the rail and looked down to the ground floor. Metal suicide netting prevented anyone from trying to defy the laws of gravity. There were cells running parallel to each other, stretching down each side of the landing. There were two or three bridges which could be walked across to get to the opposite landing and cells. This was mainly so the screws could get from side to side more easily. The last thing they wanted to do was have to gate vault the rails and run across the suicide netting to get to the other side, although I have seen that done.

Other cons were leaning over the rails, too, taking in the sight of A Wing activity. It had a profound effect on me. I never got used to the size of the place. It was ironic that the cells were tiny but the wing was huge – all noise, movement and chaos.

I looked round to see various groups of blokes on their way down, dragging their heels, chatting, laughing and being cocky. It's part of the game. Take your time getting down there so it all lasts longer. And that's the whole point inside. Make time out of your cell last longer, because the inevitable will happen during and at the end of each day: bang up.

The screws' shouts echoed around the wing, 'MOVE ON! LET'S HAVE YOU DOWNSTAIRS, PLEASE!' It was like a tape recorder of the same speech, each and every morning. The staff were on auto-pilot, many of them not even paying attention to who they were speaking to, or what exactly they said. Like the cons bunching together, the screws did much the same. They would stand there chatting, laughing and going about their business. The screws grew as much accustomed to the repetition of life inside as the cons.

Many of them had the patience of a saint. They had to, with the hassle of getting hundreds of prisoners to move their arses every day. You get a large group of adults together who all need to follow instructions, and they all slip back into child mode. You get a large group of cons and that happens, too – but with the added stress that there could be a tear up at any given time.

'Get your arse downstairs before I boot my size twelve up it, you piece of shit.' Cramfield had the manners of a pig.

I clenched my fist and gritted my teeth. I wanted to take his fucking head off. But I had bigger fish to fry. I wanted out of that nick and he wasn't going to ruin it for me.

'On me way, Guv.'

I turned on my heels and started to walk slowly towards the stairs, like every other robot. The factory line.

'That's what I thought, you fucking coward,' he tried one last time to provoke a fight.

He never got bored of bending me up. Never. He was game, though. We hated each other and he made it as clear to me as I did him, but he wasn't scared one bit. I respected him for that, at least. He wasn't a weak bully who would come mob-handed into my cell to smash me up. Sure, I'd been bent up by teams of screws hundreds of times – when I'd barricaded in my cell, causing mayhem. Screws. That's how they deal with it. It fucking hurts, but it's effective. But Cramfield never brought a mob in with him. Some screws bottle it when they have the opportunity for a straightener. Instead of sorting it out one on one when they have a problem with a con, they come back with a load of mates to watch and protect them, so that there's only one outcome. Cramfield wasn't like that. Despite all his faults, he was a man about it. He'd left me battered on the floor of my cell more than once. Likewise, he'd come in to have it out with me and left with his face rearranged and teeth missing, too. But lose or win, Cramfield kept it between us. No 'placing on report' bullshit. Everyone knew it went on but there weren't many people who would dare cross him. Cons or screws. He was a hard man, end of. His ethos was that prison should not be a nice place. Those who resided inside were entitled to fuck all.

14

As I walked down the landing, I pulled my shoulders back, head in the air, taking each step slowly.

'Yes, bruv,' Tommo touched his fist on mine as he greeted me. 'What's that prick's problem?'

'He's a bum boy; being around all these fellas is frustrating for him.'

Tommo laughed hard. He was an interesting character. A wheeler dealer, he had all ten fat little fingers tucked into every pie you can think of. He wasn't a fighter or a bully. He was astute, a businessman with a very cocky and funny manner. He finally got his conviction when he was caught bringing half a dozen truckloads of tobacco illegally into the country. He wasn't doing a short sentence either. It seems ripping off Parliament is a worse crime than being a rapist or a paedophile.

Tommo had built up a nice little enterprise on the wing. Sounds like a cliché, but this fella really could get anything. He had more than one screw in his pocket, too. He was clever, unlike the rest. He never revealed who they were. He just did what was necessary to get what he needed inside. He supplied me with all the drugs I wanted, plus the mobile phone I had hidden. He provided anything and everything.

He was a 'trusted inmate'. They're called trusted but what they should be called is extremely good at not being caught. Everyone knew what really went on. And when I say everyone, I mean the staff as well as the cons. There's no better position for a con who deals drugs to be in. When you're roaming the wing, looking busy, it's a perfect time for distribution. Tommo was a wing cleaner. Sweet.

The trusted inmates got special treatment like TVs in their cells. The majority of prisoners had to make do with a radio. And most of them didn't work. One year, Tommo made a killing trafficking handheld TVs into The Well. They may not have been a big success on the road but inside they were fucking magic. That was Tommo, always finding a gap in the market. Being locked up was an inconvenience to him but, in the end, it was just another opportunity to make some wedge.

'How we doing then, bruv? Good? You need anything, huh?'

'Cheers, Tommo, but I don't need anything. I'm outta here today.'

'Sure, blood – few beers and massage tonight then, yeah?!' Tommo laughed.

'Seriously, bruv, I'm going Clint fucking Eastwood!'

'Alcatraz, YEAH. Blut blut blut!' he said, pointing his finger at me, pretending to fire a gun. He joined me on the walk down the stairs. As we got lower to each new level, I saw the stragglers being hurried along the landing. As I got to the Twos, there was an altercation between a con and a screw.

'You take the fucking piss. You were the first person to be unlocked here, so no.'

'But I was washing, innit,' the con sucked his gums at the screw.

'You wash in your time, not mine. Behind your door.'

'Fuck you, you . . .'

He didn't get to finish the sentence. The screw grabbed him and threw him into the cell, slamming the door shut behind him. There have to be rules. Without them, people just take the piss.

I got to the ground floor. It was chaos. Cons milling about, while the officers ran around, trying to clear the landing.

'IF YOU'VE GOT YOUR MEDS, THEN OUT ON THE YARD OR BANG UP.'

From the minute you get on the landing, you hear this shouted at you but people rarely listen. It's an unspoken rule that you'll get your few minutes' morning chat before moving on. The staff are pretty good about it, as it goes. They know the best way to keep the regime on an even keel is to let the cons have a bit of give and take. As much as people might think that all the screws want to do is fight, most of them don't. They want an easy life and that doesn't include constantly rolling around on the floor with prisoners. I'm sure they accept that it might happen when they don the shirt but work is work. An operator gets bored taking calls, a cabbie gets pissed off with driving, and screws get fed up with scrapping with prisoners.

As I stepped on to the Ones, the air felt refreshing. There wasn't exactly a chill, but a minuscule breeze was blowing through the floor that I really appreciated. The door out to the yard was open and there were two officers rubbing down the inmates as they went out for exercise.

Everywhere you went, you had your body touched. They were constantly looking for weapons, drugs and God knows what else. In all honesty, they were bloody useless at it. You could have a wrap of smack in your hand and nine times out of ten, they wouldn't notice. It was just a job to these people. The effort was sometimes there, but not all the time. Complacency and boredom set in with everyone at one time or another. Every worker in the country suffers it. You end up doing the bare minimum. Screws are no different. Criminals are no different either, in fact – and that's why they get caught.

I walked through the crowd to get into the queue for medication. The queue was huge, like it was every day. The majority of the lads inside had drug habits and mental illnesses. In many cases, these problems weren't mutually exclusive, but came hand in hand with one another.

I got to the back of the queue. Tommo was already there in front of me, even though he'd been behind me all the way down. Cheeky little shit had this bounce about him; you blink, he's gone.

I'd not seen Terry since I'd left the cell. I looked up to the Fours. I saw him heading back to our cell. He noticed me looking up; he had a stoned half smile on his face but he didn't look well at all. Clearly, his breakfast of smack and weed had made the prospect exercise too much to bear. He shut the door to our cell behind him.

As I stood in queue, a few people said 'All right, Davey' or gave me 'Yes, blood' taps on the back. Mostly out of fear. I wasn't their friend. I was angry most of the time – who would want to get close to me? On the other hand, people don't like getting hurt. I was known to like to fight. So people would play the game and massage my ego so I'd leave them alone.

'Morning, Davey, how is everything?' Miss Rogers approached me as I stood there waiting. She was a very kind and sweet lady. A little younger than me, but she had an authority and confidence about her. She was very mild mannered and seemed to really care about what she was doing. She'd give you an inch, but if you tried to take any more, she wouldn't stand for it. I liked her; a lot. She always treated me with respect and dignity, even addressing me by my first name. It doesn't sound like much, but when your name is all you've got left, being spoken to like a normal person, without the usual formality, makes you feel more at ease and less aggressive. I know she used to get stick for it from her colleagues. She didn't give a toss, though, and made no effort to hide it. I had nothing but respect for her.

'Morning, Miss, I'm fine thanks. A little tired, but fine.'

She looked at me a little closer. It didn't take a genius to work out that I was blitzed out of my mind.

'I think we need to get you to see someone. You're overdoing it. If we're not careful, you'll be leaving here for the morgue.'

'I'm not that lucky, Miss. Even Him upstairs seems to want me to ride this one out!'

She gave me a concerned look. 'You know there's more to this place than . . .'

'All due respect, Miss, I don't need you preaching to me today.'

My interruption threw her a little.

'Seriously, I'm OK. This place is shit; I do my best to get through it, anyway I can.'

'You ever wanna talk, Davey . . . Look, this place can actually be a little more comfortable, if you want it to be.'

'You got a thicker mattress and aircon for me, or is it room service on offer?'

'Seriously, it doesn't have to be as tough as you make it. Lecture over.'

I stared at her for a few seconds. Some people in life truly have an angelic, selfless way about them. Miss Rogers was one of them. She walked off to help some others on the landing.

I was drawing closer to the med hatch. I started to salivate with excitement. I was about to get my daily dose of methadone. I was an addict, a junkie, after all. It was an extra chemical for my toxin-fuelled madness. The screws knew I'd become an addict since being inside, yet they still dished out the methadone. Even though I had no intention of giving up heroin, they still gave it to me. And even though I'd been inside for years, I was still given it. They knew I was still taking smack because I was still an addict; yet they still gave me my methadone. There is a fundamental flaw in the system.

Sometimes people would have their methadone stolen at the hatch. Even though it came in liquid form and you had to drink in front of the nurse, some clucking junkie or 'addict' who wanted to sell it on might still manage to steal it. Some cons would literally pounce on the lad who'd been given the small cup and take it. The nurse wouldn't say bugger all. They'd got used to it. Would let it go. Anything for a quiet life.

You'd occasionally get a new member of staff who would think they could change things. They'd bring a refreshing air of discipline, even if it was slightly annoying. It never lasted, though. They soon fell into line like every other cog in the square wheel.

A fella got to the hatch. He was clucking like mad. He looked uncomfortable in his own skin. He pulled at himself. He was covered in lesions. His eyes were glassy and had a look of pain. He stepped forward and collected the plastic beaker of methadone. I could see straight away that he was angry about the minuscule amount in front of him. He swallowed it quickly, placing the beaker back down. He stood there, waiting.

'Move on.' The nurse didn't even look at him as she dished out her orders.

'What do ya mean move on? I need some more.'

'You get what you're given. Now MOVE or I'll have you moved.'

The lad started to lose control.

'What the fuck is that little bit gonna do, huh? You even read my fucking file? You seen how much I was taking before coming here?'

That confirmed what I'd thought: new arrival. The first few days inside are extremely hard for the addict. Even if they can score some drugs, the strength is different.

'I won't tell you again, MOVE ON.'

'You call yourself a fucking nurse, you're a CUNT.' He picked up the plastic beaker and threw it at her.

He was most likely right, though. She probably hadn't checked his file.

'OFFICER, OFFICER!' she screamed. 'That man has just assaulted me!'

A plastic beaker that weighed about a gram and didn't even connect. Yeah, really bad assault.

Two screws came running over; both were fairly decent guys, as they go.

'What's going on?'

'I gave him his meds. He started screaming, then threw his beaker at me.'

Kate Winslet would have been proud.

'That true?'

'Yeah but . . .'

'No fucking buts, you mug. You get what you're given. Now move your arse.'

He was given a chance to walk away. There weren't that many screws who would have offered as much. If you're given a chance, you take it. But first timers don't really get it. They don't realise that being treated like a normal human being is taken away as well as your liberty.

'I'm not going anywhere. That fucking woman is incompetent. I wanna see a fucking doctor, right now!'

By now, we were all staring. Waiting for what was coming.

'Look, go to your cell and learn some manners,' the other screw piped up.

'Or we'll teach you some, cunt.'

They went to move him on.

'Get your hands off me!' He tried to resist.

BANG! One of the screws dropped him. Sparked him clean out. Another member of staff blew their whistle to alert the centre hub of the jail that force was being used. That is, that 'official' force was being used – in other words, that someone has been wrapped up and was going to be taken to the Seg. They shouted their location and the troops came running in full force. It's a pain in the fucking arse when that happens because everyone else gets banged up until the incident is resolved.

'GET BEHIND THE DOOR!'

A whole load of voices were shouting it out.

The screws shoved us all, pushing us behind any door that could be locked. Anyone who resisted was wrapped up. I saw two or three cons getting dropped, but that didn't concern me. Not getting my methadone did.

I got locked into the laundry with about ten other lads. Seeing that the laundry was just a converted cell with machines, it was very cramped. All I hoped was that they'll get that mug down the Seg quickly, so I can get on about my business.

They shut the spy hole, to stop us watching. We heard him scream in pain as he was carried past. A few lads kicked the door.

'Fucking mug!' shouted one of them.

We were all sweating straight away. The heat was incredible. All of us in there together, like sardines in a tin. The minutes ticked by. These incidents were normally taken care of pretty damn quick. Dropped, cuffed, carried, Seg – normal regime continues. The minutes felt like hours, though.

I was getting frustrated. I could taste the dirty damp. It was beginning to get to me. The walls started to look closer, the faces of the other lads more sinister. Staring. Looking. Fuck do they want? My fist began to clench. I didn't want them to all look at me. Talk about me. What were they laughing at? Me? I'll show them.

CRACK! The door unlocked. At last. I sighed with relief,

opened my tight fist and let the adrenaline seep out of my pores. I pushed the bloke in front of me, to hurry him along. He looked round aggressively. Once he saw it was me, he went about his business.

I stepped back on to the landing and everything carried on as normal. Just like nothing had happened. Normal. Life.

I made my way back to the med hatch. Tommo still managed to get in front of me.

'Prick should have moved on, bruv, huh?' Tommo was pissed off like the rest of us.

It's a selfish life, inside. I, like the rest, was always trying to make my own existence more palatable. For some, that meant going with the grain, living by the rules. For others, it meant finding religion or doing drugs. In most cases it was a combination of things. Anything to kill bird.

I found fighting was the answer. It gave me purpose. It gave me a reason to be behind the door. I thought that being tough, being the hardest, was what it was all about. Doing everything I shouldn't be doing gave me the power and kudos I needed. Setting my own standards was the only thing I had. I dared any bastard to take that away from me.

I nodded at Tommo's remark. I couldn't be arsed to chat. My eyes were on the hatch – the dirty, wooden hatch, with cracked varnish and metal bars over the top. To me, it was as nice a sight as the view from Kilimanjaro.

Tommo and two others were in front of me. People were

taking their meds quickly. They didn't want to piss off the miserable bitch.

Tommo got to the hatch. He looked around and saw the anguish on my face.

'There you go, bruv, you need this more than me.'

He was right, too. Tommo wasn't an addict at all. He only sold the stuff. The nurse didn't batter an eyelid. She didn't give a shit, just as long as she wasn't disturbed.

'Cheers, son.'

I necked it in one. My turn. She gave me a large beaker full. I swallowed that straight down, too.

'Miss, I got a real bad headache and I hurt my shoulder in the gym yesterday.'

I knew what to say – I had to have some sort of muscular swelling as well as the headache. That way they'd give me paracetamol for one thing and ibuprofen for the other. Any drug and every drug. It all helped.

She gave me two of each, with a small beaker of water. Down they all went.

'Thank you, Miss.'

I turned on my heels. The landing was a lot quieter by then. I heard the thumps of cell doors shutting, as the screws banged up those who refused exercise.

There were usually two reasons for refusing exercise. First, laziness: they couldn't get out of their pit in time. Second, they preferred to return to their cells after their meds so they could enjoy a little self medication as well. But, believe it or not, there weren't that many who refused exercise. It's free time out of the cage, after all.

'LAST CALL EXERCISE! OUT ON THE YARD OR BANG UP!' Mr Woodcock, the screw by the yard door, shouted up the wing.

There were still a few stragglers running around or collecting their meds. I walked up to Mr Woodcock. He was an old screw, coming to the end of his service. He didn't give a fuck. He didn't care what went on, as long as he was safe and didn't have to use too much energy – quite a common work ethic for the staff.

'Arms up, lad,' he ordered, so he could rub me down.

Each arm was rubbed with both his hands, then the chest, back and collar, around the waistband, and each leg, paying particular attention to the sock area. Some screws were more thorough at rubbing down than others.

'You on workshops today, Guv?' I asked.

'Sure am, lad.'

That was music to my ears. It's what I'd been waiting for. Planning for.

'What about Mr Jones, he with you?'

'Yep.'

'Easy day then, Guv?'

'Always, Sommers, always. Let's have you outside.'

'Sweet, Guv.'

Laurel and Hardy on the workshops – it doesn't get better than that. I'd been waiting for this day. They were two

27

dinosaurs who'd worked together for centuries and didn't give a shit.

The workshops were an opportunity to earn a few extra pence for canteen. They were situated in an outer building, on the other side of the yard. After exercise, everyone would go back inside the wing and the workshop workers would queue at the yard gate. Once the wing had been counted, they'd be sent across.

The kind of work we were given came from outside companies and was pretty basic stuff – like putting the cutlery together for pre-packed meals or joining two components of a circuit board. It's extremely cost effective for the company, plus it gets the con out of their cell, so they're happy about it, too. I'd had nearly every job in the prison, but I always cocked it up and got sacked. I was supposed to be refused entry back into the workshops. The officers on duty would have a list of names of the people who were working that day; they would tick them off each session, so they knew who was inside. Simple. But Mr Woodcock and Jones found even doing that a ball ache. So they had a first come, first served method instead. You got in the queue, you got counted through. When they had the maximum number, they locked the gate. That's the unorganised chaos of nick. If you're switched on, it's not too difficult to manoeuvre around the prison. You just need to pick the right (or wrong, depending on how you look at it) member of staff to get you where you want to be. Because the two of them were on workshops, I was going to be able to get through the gate.

I walked out on to the yard. The sun was blinding already. The humidity was thick; the air practically non-existent. Even so, it was more air than I'd had all night. It was a pleasure to feel the openness – see the sky and feel the sun touch my skin, instead of heating the walls outside of my cell.

I walked around the yard in an anti-clockwise direction, like most of the rest. Some were sitting with their tops off, enjoying the sun. Others jogged around. Some did body-weight training: press-ups, sit-ups etc. There were a few laughs and jokes. There was a weird sense of freedom out there. Especially when the weather was good. That was the worst time to be behind the door. But looking up at an open sky gave me a revved up sense of my identity returning. The natural elements always had a profound effect on me, physically and mentally.

My face broke into a small smile and I squinted my eyes. The extra blanket of calm which the med hatch had given me was serene and blissful.

'Davey boy!' Mr Wise called over to me. He was a young lad, twenty-one or twenty-two, and a fairly new screw. I liked him a lot. He was a funny guy. He took to the jail like a duck to water. He had babyish features and a lads' mag air about him. Tits and beer were his main topics of conversation. The female staff were fans. People took liberties with him, though – the other officers and some of the cons. They saw his looks and age as a weakness. But it wasn't at all. He got more shit than most because of the way he looked, but he took it well and gave as good as he got. He gained a lot of respect for the way he was. He was fair and anything but a pushover. He'd also practically saved me from bleeding to death. So you could say I had a decent relationship with him.

'Morning, Mr Wise. How's tricks?'

'Hungover but good. You?'

'Felt a bit rough earlier this morning, but more relaxed now.'

He knew full well what I was on.

'Any more, you'd be horizontal. Still, it's a better Davey that way, I guess!'

'Any crumpet last night then, Guv?' I loved to banter with him.

'Yeah, she was called Doner and came with chilli sauce!'

I carried on walking slowly. I saw Mr Jones standing with a steaming cup of coffee, looking bored. If I didn't know any better, I'd have thought he was waiting to die. Tommo had gathered a crowd round him as he told a story. He was a raconteur of the finest class. There was laughter as Tommo began to gyrate his hips and smack the air.

The yard itself was in between A and B Wing. It was used by both wings but at different times. B Wing had it in the afternoon. While we were out, the guys on B Wing would stand at their windows, shouting down to us. More often than not, we had normal chats, but sometimes it'd be a threat or similar. I was used to having abuse shouted at me from the windows. I'd made a lot of enemies.

'I'll carve you up, Sommers, you cunt.'

I didn't even flinch. It was just another piece of lunacy. It was always difficult to see where the voices came from. There were so many windows, all with external bars. I didn't bother responding – it was pointless arguing with the side of a building. You looked like a complete tosser, as well.

I carried on walking round, stopping every now and then, and soaking up the freedom.

Usually, I'd do several sets of press-ups, burpees and sit-ups. I liked to keep my body strong. As contradictory as it sounds, I liked to be fit – I didn't see the drugs as a health problem. They were just one of my bird killers. I wanted to conserve my energy, though. I'd taken more drugs than normal. I hadn't anticipated the overwhelming pressure of my nerves screaming at me. The drugs were a means to an end.

I found a spot, nicely positioned in the sun. I pulled off my sweater and vest. I looked down at my body. It was the first time I'd actually taken any notice of my shell for a long time. My torso was ravaged with battle scars from my life of crime. Inside and out. My arms, chest and back were leathery and tattooed. A mixture of dragons and old English battle proverbs. The pictures had become barely legible, the words difficult to read – a by-product of old-fashioned tattoos but it was also a visible representation of the rot inside. I had a body that was literally riddled with scars. Some of them had barely finished healing.

I'd turned forty and I was in a hellish state. A living purgatory; one that I could have clawed out of at any time but my daily helpers kept me in that bad place. I should have had a nice house, a wife and children – everything which most people take for granted. A traditional life. But I'd chosen something else.

'MAKE YOUR WAY OVER TO THE DOOR,' screamed Mr Woodcock.

My drifting thoughts had swept away my sense of time; exercise was over. We all made our way to the wing door. As we stood there, they called us in, one landing at a time. I stood waiting as the conveyor belt of activity started. The Ones, Twos, Threes were called.

'FOURS!' barked Mr Woodcock.

I made my way inside and just a few people were left out on the yard from the Fives. I made my way back up to my cell for bang up, while the screws counted the wing. Half the wing had sowsh from ten until eleven a.m., and the other half had it from eleven until twelve. The cons on workshops started at ten and didn't head back to the wing until just after twelve, when they joined the others for feeding, and then it's lunchtime bang up while the staff have lunch.

Terry was asleep when I walked into the cell. Stoned. Hammered. The door slammed behind me. The systematic echoes of all the wing doors slamming sounded like giant dominoes falling to the ground. An eerie silence followed. The screws grabbed a brew, the cons dozed for ten to fifteen until stage two of the regime commenced.

I didn't sleep, though. I needed to start the next phase of my plan. I needed to make a call on my mobile, courtesy of Tommo. Phones were only held by the top boys in prison – the price was too high for any old con to be able to have one. The top boys would lend them out to those who wished to borrow them. Payment for the privilege could be any number of things – tobacco, sweets or drugs. Sometimes it'd be in return for smashing someone up – another con or a screw. Or, maybe, you'd promise that a visitor would traffic something into the nick for them. Whatever the deal, it had to be paid in full, or skulls were cracked.

Since Tommo and I were pretty tight, when I'd told him I needed a phone – not just for one call, but as a line of communication – he didn't ask why, he just got one for me. He was happy to provide it – everyone knew I had his back. People knowing that was usually enough to keep him safe. If there ever was any threat, though, I dealt with it. That's also why he kept me loaded with as many drugs as I wanted.

Since a phone was contraband with a high net worth, I had to keep it very well hidden indeed. Not just from the burglar-screws who searched your cell, but from those who were banged up as well. You need to keep it close to you but out of sight. There is one place that is close to you. A place that is out of sight. And it's a place that no one (in their right mind) would want to go. Your arse. Perfect for keeping things you don't want found – drugs, phones and, in some cases, weapons can be hidden up there. It's amazing how people learn to adapt to their surroundings. In my heyday as a criminal before being sent down, I'd never have believed that one day I'd carry a phone and drugs up my arse.

But I needed to make a call and quick. I pulled down my jogging bottoms and pants. I squatted as low as I could. It made it easier for retrieval. Any squeamishness I'd felt when I first did it had totally gone. Now it was part of my every-day life. It was still a little painful as I pulled it out. Think brick.

Obviously, I kept it switched off when I was carrying. And I never kept any numbers saved on the phone and always deleted any calls made and received. Any text messages were also deleted. This was to protect the people I was in contact with on the outside, in case the phone was found on a cell spin or when I was taken down the Seg. Obviously some of the people I spoke to were crooks, but others weren't. Details of anyone I was speaking to would have been seriously good Intel for the Old Bill, if they'd got hold of it. Because of the organised crime I'd been involved with over the years, just the fact that someone was talking to me while I was inside would have been enough for them to receive constant tugs from the police, however innocent they were. It wasn't worth it. So, all the numbers I used were memorised.

I punched a number in.

'We on, bruv?' answered Mikey.

'It's all go. This is it. Where are ya?'

'In the café, like you said. You told me to wait there just in case . . .' He was defensive with me. He could hear the hesitation and adrenaline in my voice.

'All right, all right, I weren't getting aggro, just asking. It's on.'

'When do you want me there?'

'Fifteen, no sooner.'

'Sweet, Davey.'

'Don't sweet me, this is serious shit.' I was anxious and, as always, I took it out on someone else.

'Look, Davey, I know where to be. I'll be there.'

'Good. If I ain't there in thirty, tops, fuck off.'

'What if . . .' He was only checking things, but I wouldn't let him speak.

'No "WHAT IFS",' I shouted. Next to me, Terry jumped out of his skin. I was getting a little too vocal.

'No "what ifs",' I repeated. 'I get caught, you're hanging about, you're implicated.'

'I understand. Be lucky, son. I'll see ya on the other side.'

I hung up and stood there, contemplating what the future held. Terry looked at me, bemused.

'What's happening, Davey, huh?'

'It's fuck all to do with you, is it? Got a present for ya, though.'

I tossed him the mobile. His face lit up. It really was a gift. They were like rocking-horse shit to get hold of, and Terry was nowhere near the top of the food chain, so for him to have his own was a real treat.

I heard the cell doors beginning to crack open on my landing. The sound got louder and louder. My feet began to tap, my hands to shake. My eyelids twitched, my heart thumped. Adrenaline is the strongest chemical a body can be served. All the poison I'd pumped into myself was taken over by the alert sense of danger that my adrenal glands filled me with.

It's a fight or flight feeling. We all get it. If danger presents itself, the body's natural instinct is to fill it with adrenaline – to stay and battle, or run the other way. Do the dangerous deed or not. It's a fine balance. The flight syndrome is not always the act of a coward. Likewise, staying to fight it out, or do the robbery, be in the danger, is not always a demonstration of courage. Sometimes walking away takes the bigger man and sometimes staying in the danger is the righteous course of action. The only way to address it is first to recognise the chemical reaction that's happening and realise your thoughts will be clouded by instinct. Next you need to step out of yourself and evaluate the appropriate course: fight or flight.

My natural instinct was to fight. Always. Whatever the situation, it was punch first, think later. Sometimes I've been justified, other times I've just been flat wrong. I never recognised the chemical reaction that was happening in my body. I was a danger junkie. The excitement of fight or flight was as addictive as substance abuse. And the feeling it gives is, ironically, sobering. Even though I'd taken so many drugs that morning, as I stood there waiting for my door to open, I was more alert than ever.

'You going for a shower?' Terry asked me.

'Workshops.'

'You're banned, innit?'

'Chas and Dave are on today.'

Terry pissed himself laughing.

'You getting out of your pit?' I asked.

'Don't need to, now you given me this!'

'Put it away, you Muppet, the door will be open in a sec.'

The door cracked. I looked round at Terry.

'See you after, Tel,' I said, feeling a little nostalgic.

He gave me a thumb then got his head back down.

I moved on to the landing, looking left and right, making sure Cramfield didn't see me run downstairs to queue up for workshops. He was a permanent thorn in my side, always ready to catch me out. He was the first hurdle I needed to clear. I looked round, back and forth. He was at the other end of the landing talking to some fella, so I sprinted downstairs.

If a prisoner is somewhere they shouldn't be – like workshops when they're banned – a screw would never bother to go get you out. That's too much hassle. Far too much. They would rather scratch and sit, and dig you out upon your return. They'd never nick you for it. The Governor would laugh them out of the adjudication. Because you don't carry keys, if a con is where he shouldn't be, it's the officers who are to blame. I just needed to get there without being caught. Woodcock and Jones were a gift.

As I got to the workshops queue, it was already a substantial size. Woodcock and Jones's presence had been noticed by several others. Everyone wanted to go over to workshops with them on. They just sat there and drank tea, so cons could smoke dope, chat and drug deal without bother. They never moved from their seats unless there was any sort of violence. If that happened, the alarm would be raised and shop would be shut for the day. So it never happened when they were on because it was an easy ride. Why spoil it? If there was any violence, the con responsible would get a fucking good hiding back on the wing for it.

The queue was already so long, it was going to be touch and go whether I got through. Once Woodcock and Jones had their numbers, no one else was allowed in. I started to push forward, trying to jump a few spaces, as did some of the others. I HAD TO get through, though. I pushed two or three people out of the way, no problem. Then I came to Salty. A big Glaswegian nutcase. I'd known him for years. We'd had a run in, in my early days. I tried to get in front of him but he was having none of it.

'Touch me again, cunt, I'll rip ya heed off,' he said in his thick accent.

He had hands like shovels and thick hair all over him. His eyebrows joined in the middle, his stubble was thicker than a Brillo pad and his Popeye forearms and hands were clothed in pubic-like hair.

I had to keep any fight low key. Woodcock and Jones would jog you on if they smelt a whiff of trouble in the queue. The people standing around us who had heard Salty speak to me stood back. They thought it was going to go off. They were right. I kneed Salty in the bollocks. As he bent over in pain, I drove my knee into his face. Very hard, very fast. He fell back into the people behind him. I tried to do it as quietly and quickly as I could. But it's only so quietly that you can put someone on their arse. I thought I'd fucked up but, as he tried to scramble to his feet, a couple of lads booted him in the head, knocking him out. He lay by the wall, asleep, with the rest of the queue standing around him, hiding the view. Everyone closed ranks because they didn't want shops to be cancelled. Woodcock and Jones could have called off the whole fucking thing if they'd seen the fighting. They'd consider it unrest in the group. That was the last thing anyone wanted. I was a lucky bastard. I looked ahead.

'If you don't want the same, fucking MOVE,' I said to those in front.

It wasn't the parting of the Red Sea, but a good eight cons got out of my way. I was safe – I'd definitely be getting through.

I saw Jones on the radio asking permission to move his group of prisoners from the wing to the shops.

They unlocked the door to the yard and Jones went outside to wait, while Woodcock counted us through. One or two were refused. Fuck. Did they know what I was up to and were they waiting for me to get near so they could pounce? The voices started again. But there was more chance of Ghandi losing his rag than these two. Head down, just walk, is what I was thinking. I inched closer. They weren't even rubbing people down. Trusting, too bloody trusting. Just what I needed.

I was three away from the door when Mr Woodcock stopped the line. He turned and shouted to Jones outside.

'That's it. That's our numbers.'

The sighs of frustration were like a verbal Mexican wave. Mine wasn't a sigh, though; sheer panic was setting in. I had to get through – HAD TO. We stood there for a minute or two waiting. Hoping that Woodcock and Jones would change their minds.

'That's it, lads, back to your landing. We got our numbers.'

How could they have? I'd knocked Salty out, shoved my way up the queue, only to be told I wasn't getting through? They were a pair of lazy bastards but I never had them down as a hundred per cent incompetent. What had gone wrong?

'I've just counted. You're five short, you prick!' Mr Jones shouted back.

I could have kissed him.

As Woodcock laughed, he counted through the next five. YES. I walked on to the yard, breathing in the fresh air. Fresh probably isn't the best word to describe it. Repugnant stench is more appropriate. But, each time I walked out into the open, it smelt like the crispness of Norfolk to me. And, on that day, even more so. I could taste my freedom.

We stood just outside the door like sheep around their shepherd. Mr Woodcock was locking the gate behind us; Mr Jones was at the front waiting. I was hoping that they'd be true to form and break from procedure. One screw is supposed to walk at the front, with the cons following behind, and the second screw is supposed to walk at the back. Simple. But these two didn't like doing that. Oh no. The two-hundred-and-fifty-metre walk to the workshop was too much to bear without having a chat on the way. What they normally did, and what I was counting on, was walk together at the front of the pack.

'LET'S GO,' shouted Jones, as he started walking.

Woodcock was still at the rear. I looked round, but all he was doing was fiddling with his balls and scratching his arse. Nice. Back and forth I swung my head, willing the daft old sod to do his usual. The metres were ticking down. We were getting closer to the workshops. Fuck.

'Mr Jones,' he shouted, 'wait up!'

He waddle-jogged past me and the rest of the group. YES.

I started drifting towards the back. The other cons were too scared of me to talk – people only spoke to me when I spoke to them. If I didn't, they left well alone. Which was lucky – the last thing I needed was someone making idle chit chat. I was concentrating so hard, it was literally hurting.

The group started to drag their heels a little, enjoying the stroll. Every now and then Jones and Woodcock would shout a token, 'KEEP UP', and the group would close the gap between them ever so slightly. But not me. I wanted that gap. We were approaching the workshop and I was a fair distance behind the group; and even further behind Chas and Dave at the front.

The workshop was a brick warehouse that had only one floor. It had very small windows, all covered with bars. Most of the light inside was light-bulb generated. It had one way in, and one way out. There was a fire exit at one end, which hadn't been unlocked since the day it was built. There were bins and a whole host of crap that lined the outside walls. Just next to the workshop was a fifteen-foot pole, like a lamppost but thinner, and there was a CCTV camera on the top. Just behind it was the perimeter wall, which was about five feet taller. The size of both the pole and the wall were bigger than I had remembered, even though I'd studied them for more than two months.

Everyone was heading to the right where the front door of the building was. Not me. I drifted to the left. I wanted to get lost among the crap that lined the workshop wall. More importantly, I needed to get close to the camera pole. I needed to make a quick dash away from the group and into the comfort of the shadows. I made more than one false attempt – it must have looked as if I had the worst tick known to man. Thankfully, no one was looking at me or giving a fuck. The shop was getting ever closer. I had to make a break for it, or it was all over . . . GO!

I sprinted like a maniac. I held my breath the whole time, praying that no one from the cells would notice and scream out the window at me below. I had to rely on luck. It must have been a hundred feet, tops, but it felt like a thousand miles.

Finally, I reached the wall and hid behind two wheelie bins that were surrounded by cardboard and overflowing with shit. I was panting so hard I nearly passed out. The lads continued on their walk. I stared out through a gap, watching as they made their way to the door. I felt something on my foot. I looked down and saw a rabbit. Only that's not what it was. A RAT. A fucking rodent the size of a rabbit had just run over my foot. It had no fear whatsoever. But I did. I kicked it hard and jumped back, scrambling to get away. If I could have pushed the wall down and climbed into the workshop, I would have. All that planning and risk destroyed by a rat. A fucking rat. I kicked it a couple of times more before it retreated. Whether it was the drugs or the adrenaline, I swear that bastard growled at me.

I'd pushed against the bins and made some noise in the process. Somehow, I'd managed to keep my gob shut, though. The brain is an incredible organ; even in situations of discomfort and danger, it is still in control. Even in my terrified state, I somehow knew that if I shouted, I was busted for sure. I quickly looked to assess if anyone had noticed. They hadn't. They were all still walking towards the door. In fact, most of them were out of sight now and inside.

Once inside the workshop, the screws are supposed to count the cons again. Jones and Woodcock never did, though. But I couldn't be sure they wouldn't this time. If they did, I'd have to run over and make up some bullshit about how I'd gone for a piss, or something. I needed to know that they hadn't noticed my disappearance from the group before I could go any further. I couldn't risk being caught halfway through.

I watched as the last one went out of sight. I bit my knuckle, breathing fast. I was waiting for that door to slam and the key to turn. Come on, come on.

BANG, CLUNK. YES. I was on the out.

I reached into my jogging bottoms and pulled out an inch-long glue stick from a hole in my waistband. It was the glue from a Pritt Stick. I fucking loved Tommo; gets you anything. I rubbed it all over both my hands. I didn't think it was going to give me that much more traction for climbing, but it made me feel better.

It was a tall order, climbing a CCTV pole. Madness. But what did I have to lose? Not my liberty. I was hell bent on getting out of prison. And since there hadn't been an escape for over twenty-seven years, I knew it wasn't going to be easy.

I looked left and right. No more time to psyche up. I sprinted to the pole. It was only twenty feet away. I jumped on to it. It was rusty and just the right thickness to grab. Perfect. I started climbing it like a rope. It was tough. I put the soles of my feet on there, too, and monkey climbed. I switched from one way of climbing to the other a few times. As I made my way up, I could see the CCTV camera on the top. You'd think that I might have been seen on the camera. Sure, there was an outside chance. But it was common knowledge that the screws on camera watch normally got their heads down instead. No one tries to escape, so why watch? Plus, the tape would be there to look at afterwards, if evidence was ever needed. A shift on the cameras was cushy for the lazy civil servant.

I got to the top within seconds. Now I had to wrap myself around the camera and the top of the pole in such a way that I could push off from it and give myself enough power to jump from the pole to the top of the wall. I also needed something to grab hold of when I landed. That, I'd worked out, was staring right at me. The barbed razor wire. That was the way my mind worked. Don't see a physical deterrent as a hindrance, but as an aide. Of course, I knew it would hack my hands, and potentially my body, to pieces. But it was a small price to pay to be free.

I curled myself around the pole like a cat, counted to three and jumped. That quick. I couldn't hesitate. If I had done, I might have lost my bottle.

As my hands hit the wire, I felt a squelch, as if a water-filled balloon had burst. Blood dripped down as my flesh ripped apart. I pulled myself on to the wall top and into the wire. I had puncture holes and rips all the way up my torso. It was tearing me apart. But I felt no pain. Nothing.

It had cost me some blood and it was going to hurt when the adrenaline wore off, but I was on the top.

That's when I noticed Mikey sitting down below in his car. He looked up at me through the window. The drop was bigger on the other side. I was sure I'd bust my legs, but it was worth it. I was about to throw myself off when Mikey jumped out of the car.

'LAMPPOST!' he screamed, pointing at one just a few metres away. It was fairly thin and it was lower than the wall, so it was going to take some skill and a lot of luck to reach it.

I jumped into it and slipped down, like a bloody piece of

dead meat. I hit the ground but, surprisingly, not too hard. I'd broken my wrist, but my legs were OK.

Mikey helped me to my feet and shoved me into the passenger seat of his motor. He jumped in and we sped off.

'You're one crazy cunt, Davey Sommers!' he said laughing.

I was delirious. I couldn't take in what I'd just done. Inexplicably, instead of feeling euphoric, I felt empty. Ill. I'd just stolen back my liberty but I was soon to learn that I was anything but free . . .

A CLOCKWORK GUN

'**M**ake the tea, then, if I'm going to cook this for you!' said Mum, as she fried a Sunday breakfast.

I put the kettle on. It was already light; the dew smelt fresh and the birds chirped, even though it was only just after five a.m.

'It's nice to see you up this early, David, but what is it you're doing today again?' She was still half asleep and asking the same question over and over. But then, having your eighteen-year-old son wake you up to ask for some breakfast at that hour on a Sunday morning wasn't ordinary behaviour.

I wasn't ordinary. I was just beginning to learn my trade.

Crime. By the age of eighteen, I wasn't a 'no mark' anymore. I was starting to make waves in the way I handled and conducted myself. More importantly, though, in the way I handled others; in particular, those who needed handling.

'Told ya, Mum, I'm playing football,' I laughed. 'Gotta keep up my strength for it, huh?'

She squinted her eyes at me and shook her head. Mum wasn't daft. She knew I was naughty. Into things I shouldn't be. She and Dad always tried to steer me in the right direction, but, what is right? I'm not saying the path I chose was particularly good, but it was what I was made for. It was part of my makeup. It was the path I was born to follow.

The smell of the crispy bacon filled the kitchen. The crackling noise of it frying in the pan always made me feel like a child. Protected and looked after. I sat at the table and watched Mum tentatively turn the food as it cooked. Unconditional love. Five in the morning and there she was, up and cooking a breakfast for her son. I could always count on her, day and night.

Dad normally got up around seven-thirty on a Sunday. He'd prepare for Sunday service, have breakfast and then head to church. I don't want to paint my dad as some sort of Bible basher – Benjamin Sommers was anything but that, in many respects. He'd been in the Army, was a terrific boxer and loved everything any regular bloke would. But he had found his 'calling' and become a pastor. His was a free church – non-prejudicial on denomination and background.

The smell of the bacon and the subtle sounds of the radio were enough to get my dad out of bed.

'Blimey, you two are up early!' he said, as he walked into the kitchen.

'David's playing football today. He wanted a feed before he left.'

Dad looked at me sitting at the table. My smile started to falter. Mum wasn't stupid, like I said, but Dad was switched on. There's a difference. Just because he was a pastor doesn't mean he was blind to the realities of life and what went on in the streets. He was a tough cookie and couldn't be fooled easily.

As he looked at me, I could see him clocking my attire. Heavy boots, blue jeans and a lumberjack shirt. On the table was a pair of fingerless leather gloves, a fishing knife and my two-piece snooker cue in its leather case.

'Mmm, that's some strange equipment you've got there for a game of football, isn't it, David?'

'Er . . .well, we might be . . .' I coughed to buy some time, 'might be going fishing as well. And the cue's Donnie's. He wants it back.'

He could see straight through me.

'He wants to play snooker at five in the morning on a Sunday, does he?' Dad said, sarcastically.

Mum could see a row coming.

'How many eggs, love?' she half shouted it at me, to try and defuse the tense atmosphere.

'Two please, Mum.'

Dad just stared. He had this way of looking straight through my outer shell. He knew what I was about, I could see that.

'Ben, what would you like, love?'

'Egg and tomato on toast please, Millie.' He didn't take his eyes off me as he answered Mum. 'You just be careful, David. You know that we all have a purpose; just make sure you're trying to find yours.'

He sat down. His words resonated with me. I understood what he was saying. But I chose to put them to the back of my mind and forget them for now. That much, I did have in common with other eighteen year olds.

Adam came walking into the kitchen, rubbing his eyes, wearing just his boxer shorts.

'What the fuck is going on so early?'

'ADAM, watch your language!' Mum shouted.

'Sorry, Mum.'

Adam came and sat next to me. He was back from uni for the weekend. He stank like a brewery. He'd been out on the piss the whole weekend. He was three years older than me and flying. He was training to be a doctor and was doing a bloody good job, by all accounts. He was extremely bright. He knew how to play the game well. He enjoyed himself; make no mistake about it, though. Purple hearts and barrels of Guinness. He was good with the ladies as well. But he had the balance right. He was always organised and knew what needed to be done to succeed. He didn't waste the minutes he was given. Adam was clever. Although we didn't see each other all that often, we were still very close and good mates. When he wanted some speed or acid, I would sort him out. Brotherly love.

'The fuck you doing up so early, mate?' he whispered to me.

I looked over to Dad. He was reading yesterday's paper. Adam and I were huddled close together.

'Got a bit of business to attend to,' I answered.

'This early on Sunday?'

'I ain't trading in the city, am I, you Muppet! I've got to know the associates I'm dealing with are at home. No better time than now.'

Mum put a plate of food in front of me; two eggs, three rashers, two sausages, beans and a fried slice. I shovelled it in. Perfect. Belly full, I picked up my tools.

'Cheers, Mum. Right, I'm off. I'll see ya later.'

Dad looked at me, concerned.

'Take it easy, bruv,' Adam said.

'You back for . . .'

I slammed the door shut behind me, cutting Mum's question off.

I didn't have too far to get to Donnie's gaff. He lived just around the corner. He was my best pal. We did most things together. We were part of a group of teenagers (girls and boys) that hung around, getting stoned, high and pissed, and shagging all the time.

Donnie and I were the ones that got hold of the chemicals of choice. Acid, speed and weed were the drugs we used recreationally. Donnie and I liaised with the dealers – two blokes in their twenties who acted Billy Big Bollocks to a group of teenagers. They were a pair of wannabe gangsters. Don't get me wrong; as far as most people were concerned, they were a couple of dangerous blokes. But Donnie and I always felt that, one day, we would take their places. They were a pair of stupid bastards, in all honesty. They had a nice big flat, which they dealt from. It had a kind of open house policy, especially at the weekend. It was like one big party that went on for three days. The group Donnie and I ran with didn't have the balls to go there, but we did.

I wasn't going to take all the risks for nothing, though, so we put a price on top of what we were paying for the drugs. Before long, friends of friends wanted some and they were coming to Donnie and me. Drug dealing: that's how it starts. We were beginning to make a mint. A lot more than I was getting as an apprentice telecom engineer; a job that I hated. I didn't have it in me to carry around a tool box to make a living. There was nothing in it that provided me with excitement or the prospect of utilising my natural skills. I hardly ever went into work anyway. I knew the sack was coming, but I didn't give a fuck. Instead, I spent my time learning my real trade and making a shit load of dough in the process.

A few weeks earlier, Donnie and I were coming out of an off licence, when we were approached by a big, black geezer. An imposing man who had burn marks on the left side of his face and his eye missing on that side. He was one scary-looking bastard.

'Yes, lads, a word, if I can.'

Donnie and I looked at each other; we were too scared to say no. We went over to him in a dark space between the off licence and the kebab shop next door.

'You boys know who I am?'

'No.' I did the talking.

'Well, my name's Casey, and I'm in charge of what gets sold in this town. This town and several fucking others.' He started to get aggressive. 'And I don't take kindly to cunts selling drugs behind my back.'

No two ways about it, I shat myself. But fight or flight.

'Well, Casey, I don't know who the fuck you are, or who you control. And, if I'm honest, I don't give a fuck either.' Fearful words of anger. That's how people get killed. Walk away. WALK AWAY.

Casey started to laugh.

'Calm down, I've noticed what you've been up to but I like the way you handle yourself. It's not you I've got a problem with.'

'What is it you want?' This had to be leading somewhere.

'I would like you two to come work for me. Make some real money. But it comes with a condition. I need them pair of cunts you get your gear off taken out.'

'Nah, that's not anything we're interested in.'

'Let me put it another way, Davey.' Bastard knew my name. 'You either take out or get taken out.'

He moved his long black leather coat away from his waist, revealing a pistol tucked into his trousers. It was the first time I'd seen a gun. Eighteen years old.

'What do you want us to do?' I was excited. It was the calling to the next level I'd been looking for.

'Get all their drugs, money and close shop. Easy, huh?' He started to laugh. 'Can you handle it?' he asked.

I had to think. Was I going to take a kicking, give this nutcase my money, drugs and walk in fear? Or was I going to embrace Casey?

'Yeah, we can sort it. Leave it to us.' Donnie looked at me like I was mad.

'There you go.' He gave us a wad of cash.

He wrote down his phone number and where we could find him. He made it clear he knew where we lived and who we were.

I'd accepted the work, initiation was over.

As I headed to Donnie's, I felt bloated and sweaty from the breakfast I'd had. My stomach started to make all sorts of noises. I ran the rest of the way with my cue in one hand and my arse cupped with the other.

'Donnie. DONNIE!' I shouted, as I banged on his door.

'Shut your fuckin' row, my mum's in bed. She'll go mental if she finds out what's going on.'

'I'm gonna shit myself!' I pleaded.

I ran to the bog. I don't know if it was the food or the adrenaline, but the breakfast went through me like an Aston Martin.

Donnie was dressed and ready when I came out, looking wide awake and full of anxiety.

'You OK, son?' I asked.

'Yeah, but couldn't sleep last night. Nervous, mate, nervous.'

'Did you not have a smoke?'

'Yeah, it made me more fucking paranoid!'

I looked at my watch, it was six-fifteen.

'We need to get this done, mucker, before it gets too late.'

He nodded. I checked that my knife was still secure on my belt. I took out the bottom half of my snooker queue. The heavy part. I put on my leather gloves. They weren't necessary but they made me feel a bit more bad ass. Cool. James Dean. What a prick.

Donnie picked up his weapon of choice – a cricket bat that he'd sawn in half. He'd sanded the end, varnished it, then wrapped it in electrical tape. It was like a caveman's club. Perfect job.

He grabbed the keys to his mum's car. No more walking. Bonus. We got in. Donnie put on 'Who Are You?' by The Who. He played it really loud. I don't think he could take the silence. I've still got a great fondness for that song.

We pulled into the car park of the flats. They were two-storey council flats. Our target was on the bottom. We took a couple of deep breaths.

'Ready, mate?' I asked.

'Let's just get this over and fucking done with.'

We got out of the car, concealing our weapons as much as we could. Not that there was anyone to hide them from. It was dead quiet. Peaceful. We had to look out for any old dears taking a morning walk with their dog or going to collect their papers. Thankfully there wasn't anyone about.

The door to the building was always on the latch. We walked through, getting closer to the door of the flat. You could feel the gentle thumps of Bob Marley being played on the stereo.

I put my ear to the door, trying to work out roughly how busy it was in there. The party goes on and on. Drug- and booze-fuelled weekend mayhem. I knew that this time on a Sunday morning was likely to be the most spaced-out period. Perfect for a hit. I knocked on the door.

'Who is it?' asked a female voice. I recognised it as one of their girlfriends.

'Davey and Donnie. All right for a spend?'

She unlocked the door and let us in.

The whole place was filled with smoke to the max. It stung my eyes and the sweet, sickly taste hit the back of my throat. I had the cue end held behind me. Donnie brought up the rear.

She led me down the hallway. I looked into the kitchen – a bloke was asleep on the table, next to a huge bong. She led me into the lounge. There were five people in there and a load of speed on the table, racked up in lines.

One of the dealers looked round at me.

'Davey, what can I do you . . .'

WHACK! I smashed him over the head with my cue, knocking him to the floor. Donnie ran round me, clubbing some bloke who jumped up and tried to join in. The girl who brought us in screamed. Donnie pushed her on to the sofa.

'Shut your mouth and no one else gets hurt,' he said.

I looked down at the bloke I'd smashed. He was still conscious, rubbing the top of his head. Blood had soaked his hair and was running down his temple.

'Your money and your gear. I want it. NOW.' I didn't mess around.

'The fuck you talking about? You nuts?'

I started booting him, showing I wasn't there to play.

'Look, you cunt, I won't ask twice. I'm here to take shop. You're closed for trade. It's game over. Understand?'

Some bloke got up off the sofa. He obviously wanted to be anywhere but there. His arse had totally gone. He was there for the party and getting out of his nut, having fun, and all of a sudden he's faced with two lunatics. Fuck that when you're tripping out of your mind and speeding like a locomotive.

Donnie smacked him in the gob.

'Sit the fuck DOWN.'

'This is going to be quick and easy, or long and painful. Don't fucking move and this will be over soon. UNDERSTAND?' I addressed the room.

No more movement or pissing about. I'd gone there to take over. And that's what I intended to do. Everyone nodded and sat still.

'Now, move yourself and get what's mine.' The blood was still seeping out, as I barked my order at him.

He emptied his pockets and slowly passed me all the drugs about his person. He started to crawl over to the cupboard in the corner.

'I ain't got all fucking day, you mug.' I grabbed and shoved him in the right direction.

'Not so fuckin' big now, are you? CUNT.' I couldn't help myself. The power was mine for the taking. This guy was a bully. A degenerate. But I was taking over. Somehow, in my screwed-up logic, I thought I was the saviour of drug dealing. I felt like the Richard Branson of the underworld. It was like the bank had given me the green light on my new venture and this was my first day of trading. I was excited; almost turned on by it.

He undid the cupboard and started pulling out more

money and drugs. I couldn't believe how easy it was. A bit of muscle and they melted.

'ARGH!' Donnie screamed.

I turned round to see some bloke setting about Donnie with a hammer. He was charged up. It was the guy who'd been asleep in the kitchen. The other one of this duo of dealers. We should have paid more attention to him. You live and learn.

I stepped into him, swinging my cue with all my might. With the accuracy of a sniper, he managed to knock it out of my hand.

'You come in here, you CUNTS. ROB US? I'LL KILL YOU!'

He came for me. I pulled my knife from my belt. He swung at me and I managed to dodge. Just. I sunk the blade deep into his shoulder. All the way in until only the handle was outside his flesh. He dropped the hammer and fell to his knees. I got to work on his face, punching him with everything I had. I didn't stop until he couldn't defend himself anymore and I was breathless from my savage attack. He was soaked in his own blood and unconscious. I looked around and saw the fear on everyone's faces. Including Donnie's.

'What? Get the fucking stuff, yeah?' I was panting as if I'd just finished a marathon.

Donnie snapped out of zombie mode. He went over to the fella who was getting us the gear. He was staring in horror like the rest of them. I'm not condoning my actions, but that madman came at me with a hammer. Some might say I'd given him reason. Perhaps I had. But I had to defend myself.

The two of them had been playing at being gangsters. Pretending to be the men about town. Acting tough in front of a group of teenagers. You deal in drugs, you play at crime, and the consequence is violence. Plain and simple. You mess with the underworld, and expect to hurt, or be hurt. I learned that in my first raid, there and then. It WILL catch up with you. There is always someone out there who will be willing to take everything from you by force. He may be an experienced killer or just a quick learner, like I was, but be sure of this: he is coming. Know that, accept it. If you can't, get your national insurance number and your tax code and get out.

'You – give me your bag.' I noticed some girl had a handbag the size of a suitcase.

I emptied all her crap on the floor and threw the bag at the dealer.

'Put all the dough and gear in there,' I shouted.

He didn't hesitate. He passed it to me, filled to the brim. There was still a lot that wouldn't fit in – he went on to fill three Tesco carrier bags as well.

'You listen to me, mug. SHOP'S SHUT. Casey is taking all of this and we're here to make that happen. If we catch you at it anymore . . .'

Donnie interrupted me, 'We'll be back with a shooter.' He was smirking as he said it. He had begun to enjoy our new status, as had I. We were in control and wanting to exploit that as much as we could. We'd only seen a gun for the first time a few days earlier. But we felt like big men. REAL gangsters.

'Any you cunts say anything. DEAD.' I thought I was the fucking Don.

We left the flat and headed back to our car. We were wired – shocked at what we'd just accomplished but on fire. I'd found my niche. Eighteen years old and I was on the path of the unrighteous. I couldn't have been happier.

I walked up to the desk. There was a pretty girl sitting there looking uninterested and bored.

'All right, darling, I'm here to see Casey.'

'Don't you darling me, you little cunt. Fuck off over there and I'll ring him.' Pretty, but the mouth and mannerisms of a sewer. Working on Sunday night, in a seedy, horrible club had obviously taken its toll. 'Go into the bar. He's waiting.'

'Whereabouts?' Donnie asked.

'Do I look like Superwoman? Stupid prick.' Pleasant.

We walked through to see the dredges of society, drinking and roaming around. Scumbags. Tarts cavorting around old sweats with fat wallets. The smell of Brut, stale beer and cheap cigar smoke was one I was soon to get used to. Davey Sommers, this is your life.

Beady eyes hit us as we scrambled through the illegal drinking hole. And it really was a hole. Casey stood at the bar, sipping a large rum and Coke. He had shades on. Shades in a club. At least his missing eye was covered up. He wore a tight, red roll-neck and had thick, gold jewellery hanging on his large frame.

That's when I noticed how we must have looked. Sure we were new, unrecognisable to many, but we also had three Tesco carrier bags full of money and drugs, and a large handbag about our persons.

'Casey, we shut them down. Here's all the gear and dough.'

He looked at me as I handed it over. He looked into the bags and gave me one of them back.

'What's this for?'

'Your payment, and some gear for you to sell.'

I was confused. 'How's this work?'

'You sell, then bring me the money you make. I pay and give you more.' He started to laugh.

'OK, sounds good. That it?' I asked.

'For now. But seeing as you did this job so easily, I might just call on you for a few other errands. You two are crazy kids, by all accounts. I never thought you'd have the bollocks to go through with it. Figured I'd be giving you a slap and doing it myself. You proved me wrong. BIG TIME. I love it when I find hungry pups, ready for action.'

What a conceited piece of shit. I wanted to punch his patronising words down his throat. I hated being talked down to. But I knew I'd have to accept it for now. FOR NOW.

'Nice, Casey. See you later, yeah.'

We headed out of the club. Would I stay in someone's pocket? No. I was already plotting my next step towards underworld supremacy. I was the one with big pockets and I was about to start filling them . . .

LORD, DON'T SLOW
ME DOWN

'**Y**ou come in here with a stinking fucking attitude, then have the nerve to try and knock me on the price. That's bad manners.' It was something I'd got used to saying.

I stood in one of my lock ups, face to face with a buyer of 100,000 ecstasy pills. He wasn't alone. But then neither was I. I could have let one of my blokes do the negotiations. In the twelve years since being taken on by Casey, I'd built an empire and taken out every other competitor in the process. But I never let the deals run without me. I didn't trust anyone to do it the way I could. I was loyal to myself and trusted no one else with my money. That's why I was successful.

'Davey, look, I've got overheads. I gotta get these pills out to my guys, then they gotta be put into the clubs, raves and everything else. If I don't make a price, it's not worth my hassle.'

'I know how it fucking works. How do you think I got to dealing to wankers like you, huh? By starting at ground level, working my way up. You have to make it work. That's the art of good business. Now look, you ain't gotta buy my pills, but let me tell you this, you ain't never gonna sell any again, either.' I pulled out a revolver and the guys with me cocked and pointed their semi-automatic machine guns at my wavering customer and his associates.

'WHOA, WHOA, WHOA. Take a step back, huh? No need for the guns.' He was shitting himself.

'No need for the guns, huh? FUCK YOU. Deal's off. But you're still gonna pay. Oh yes.'

He looked at me confused.

I'd never intended to sell him the pills. I already had a network of dealers placed at several raves and festivals happening over the next weekend. Dreamscape, Mindwarp, Raven – even rock festivals like Reading had started to enjoy the new drug ecstasy and I was one of the chief suppliers. I had runners and dealers working for me in every corner of the country. Cocaine had had an influx of popularity, too, but mainly with the glitterati. A ponce's powder. All of your city workers liked a sniff. Heroin had been a big phenomenon a few years earlier – but it was phasing out.

Pills and coke were the new big things. They say it was the law that tightened up on football hooliganism and made the terraces safer. OK, it played a part, but ecstasy was the real reason. Everyone just wanted to kiss each other.

They were serious money makers. There was big, big money in Es. My clients were from every social background – I had your working-class painter and decorator, your lawyers, cabbies, even some coppers and screws – they all came to me for the same reason. They loved to get high.

The rave scene may be fun for the end user, but, behind the scenes, the industry is riddled with fury and vengeance. There was a turf war for the suppliers. Insurance companies advertise on TV to get new customers, drug suppliers shoot each other to steal theirs. Regular users didn't care who they bought it off, as long as they got what they wanted. But I cared who they bought it from. I cared very much.

The bloke standing in front of me in my lock up was no more than a rival I needed to squash.

You see, that's what I did. I eliminated people. I got them out of the way.

'What do you mean, I'm still gonna pay?' His arse was twitching.

'The fucking lot, my son. Everything you've got. I'm shutting shop. You're finished around here, you get me?'

'Hang on a minute. You invited me here to buy some pills. I thought we were gonna be business partners?' He was worried. WORRIED.

Donnie stepped forward, laughing his nuts off. Before the bloke saw what was coming, Donnie had smashed him in the side of the face with the butt of his gun.

'You ain't a partner, you're a fucking WORM!' Donnie screamed.

One of his firm stepped up to Donnie.

'Wouldn't do that, sunshine.' I pointed my gun straight at his head.

'Look, Davey, this is getting out of hand. How about I move areas or something; take my crew a bit further afield?' He was rubbing his head. He was in pain. FEAR.

'You ain't listening to me, are ya? Shop's shut. Game over. You either walk away from this, or you don't. Either way, this is over for you. I'm taking the lot.'

And that's how I went on. Every firm and crew in the area and just outside, I would befriend, especially if I saw them as a threat. Then I would use force to shut them down. Take over. That's how my network grew. But I made some enemies. The worst kind imaginable. Fucking over Casey was an integral part of my success but I knew it was also something that was going to bite me in the arse when I least expected it. His was the hand that fed me. But I was hungry, so I bit it off. Loyalty is a weakness in the underworld. That's not how you get to the top of the tree. And it's a lonely and dangerous existence. Donnie was the only person I trusted, the only person in my line of work I could trust. I had a few straight friends and I was still very close to my family but there was no hiding my activities. I was a flash bastard who was happy to let people know what I was about. Not the ins and outs, of course, but I was happy for people to know I was pretty near the top of the violent food chain.

I thought I was invincible. No one could touch me. All those years in the crime business, I'd not so much as had a tug by police. Davey Sommers was the man. Gelled back hair, a sharp suit and Italian shoes. Yeah, I looked the part of a rich businessman, but I was a thug. An animal.

'Your bags, your wallets, the fucking lot, hand it over,' I ordered.

They all looked at each other, not believing what was happening. They'd come to buy drugs and now they were being taken the fuck out. They were fairly high up the chain so probably assumed they were well connected and were feared enough to be safe in the business. They knew my firm controlled a lot of what went on but they never thought I would shut them down. They assumed I'd want to sell to them and keep them going. But I did things differently. True, I could have made some money that way, but I could make shit loads more if I took their trade and put my lads on their patch. That's why I had more money than I knew what to do with.

And it wasn't just drugs and violence I was into. I had my fat fingers and toes in hundreds of pies. I owned a little independent estate agents – it looked good for the tax return. Besides, there was lots of tax-free money to be earned, helping out the cash-rich property developers. I didn't discriminate either. I would do six-figure drug deals, take bucket loads of cash from dodgy developers and still knock out stolen stereos for fifty quid. I never let go of the small things. The pennies look after the pounds, and all that.

'Look at each other all ya want, but you better hand it over right now or I'm FUCKING TAKING IT.' I'd given them a minute for it to sink in, enough was enough.

They started throwing over their wallets, plus a bag they had full of cash.

'Watches, as well.'

'You are one dirty CUNT, Sommers.' He couldn't believe how low I would go.

'See it as a lesson. Wherever it is you move to – and I'm sure you will start up again – now you'll know how it should be done.'

He stared daggers at me. I could see he wanted to rip my heart out. He couldn't believe I was that shameless.

'Right, you lot, fuck off. If I see any you cunts round here again, you'll be thrown in the fucking river. You get me?'

They nodded. They knew it was all over.

'First things first, though. Me and you are going for a drive.'

The head of the gang looked at me, confused.

'What the fuck for?'

'To get everything else that's mine. We're going to your gaff.' I was going to clear him out of money and drugs and anything else I could get my hands on. 'Donnie, you stay here with the lads and look after this lot.'

I led him out to his Range Rover that was parked outside. I still had my gun in my hand. Daylight, and there I was, walking around with a gun in my hand, without a care in the world. I was untouchable; I could do anything I wanted.

We got into the car and I noticed some blood dripping down his face from when Donnie had cracked him one. I pulled out my hanky and passed it to him.

'Here, you're bleeding.'

'Fuck you, Sommers.'

'Don't make me out to be a monster. It's business. You should have accepted the career drawbacks when you started dealing.'

Half of what I said was true. Being fucked over is a career hazard. But I was a monster. I was unpredictable. One minute I was ruthless, the next I was talking to my enemies with respect. I sent out mixed messages, which is why no one ever knew where they stood with me. And that included guys on my firm. I wouldn't hesitate to smash one of their heads in, if I thought they'd taken the piss or done something that cost me money.

I had a vicious temper. A split personality. I'd already started getting terrible headaches and the voice of hate in my mind just got louder and louder. I was smoking a tremendous amount of weed – smoking it like cigarettes – and that didn't help my state of mind. I would occasionally take Es but they were not really my cup of tea. I took cocaine recreationally – it was part of the image. It was only the rich that sniffed. I wanted to play the part of the city glitterati. I was by no means an addict, but I was quite a heavy user. I never touched smack and crack, though.

We started to drive off in his motor. I lit a cigar. Thirty years old and I was smoking a cigar. What a cock. He was silent as he drove.

'Besides being good at the business, you know what makes me good at all of this? I never get caught. I've got everyone in my pocket, and those who ain't are too scared to nick me.'

'Look, Davey, I don't give a fuck about you, so stop talking to me.'

I stared at him. The voice in my head shouted, 'Burn him. BURN HIM.' I fought with my wrist, to stop myself from doing it.

'You think you're above it but trust me, you ain't.'

BURN THE CUNT . . . NOW. I couldn't resist it any longer; I stubbed my cigar out on his neck.

'ARGHH!' he screamed, as we skidded all over the road.

I started to punch him, repeatedly. He screeched the brakes and we crashed.

'You mind your fucking MANNERS!' I screamed. 'Or I'll put a bullet in your fucking nut right now, cos I don't give a fuck.'

He cowered like a scared child.

'All right, all right,' he pleaded, 'I'm sorry, let's just get this done.'

There was a sticky blood circle on his neck from the burn and his face was swollen from my punches. He was breathing heavily.

'What you waiting for? If you swing past McDonald's on the way, I'll get us some food.' Mad.

We pulled up at his house; an end terrace in an average part of town. I was finishing my Big Mac. He hadn't wanted anything to eat, funnily enough. We got out of the car, not saying a word. There was no conversation left. Everything that needed to be said, had been.

He slowly put his key in the door and hesitated.

'Don't you even fucking think about doing anything stupid.' I pressed my gun into his side.

'I'm not. I'm about to lose everything. Whatever that is to you, it's fucking hard for me.'

'Fair point. Just get a move on, yeah.'

We walked inside. It was a pleasant place. Had a fresh smell of Glade. The carpets were clean. We walked into the lounge. A large TV sat in the corner, with thousands of videos neatly placed around it. The sofa was leather, dark brown and obviously expensive.

'Right, get the money and gear. Don't you miss any of it.'

'I get the message.'

He had an empty sports bag which he began to fill. There were all sorts of hiding places in the house and he took me to them all. Behind cupboards, under floorboards, behind light switches – he was better than I thought. But he still gave me everything. We were only in there for about twenty minutes and I cleared him out of fifteen grand in cash, two kilos of cocaine and ten thousand pills.

'You clear what you gotta do now, yeah?' I needed to be sure that he was going to disappear.

'Crystal.'

We walked outside, slamming the door behind us.

'PUT THE FUCKING GUN ON THE FLOOR, NOW!' I heard someone scream.

'What the FUCK?' I couldn't believe what was happening.

'Don't SHOOT!' the fella I was with screamed.

'GUN ON THE FLOOR NOW! FUCKING NOW!'

I was surrounded by an armed response unit. The filth. I didn't stand a chance. Even I knew that I was busted. I was dropping my gun when, BANG! I'd been shot. I felt like someone had punched me in the guts. It knocked me off my feet. The air left my lungs and, as my head hit the ground, I looked up and the world around me went into a purple haze . . .

THE FILTH AND THE FURY

'All I want is something to fucking eat. Can't you cunts at least give me that?' I was hungry. Really hungry.

'Watch your fucking manners, you mouthy cunt, or we'll smash you.' Police at their friendliest.

I don't know why I wanted the food in that hospital anyway. It was fucking disgusting. And it wouldn't have filled a sparrow. But I needed something. All the medication I was on, I felt sick, dizzy, almost like I had vertigo. My mouth was dry. I would have murdered for some water.

I was in a room on my own. I had armed guards outside and a couple of coppers in with me. I'd been in for a few days since I was shot. I was a lucky lad; the bullet went in my side, right in a fleshy part, and straight out the back. It missed all my organs and was just a flesh wound.

I didn't feel lucky, though. The pain was excruciating. I was being pumped full of painkillers and antibiotics due to an infection I'd picked up from the wound. I needed a lot of water and plenty of food but any food and drink they brought to me didn't get past the coppers. They took great pleasure in eating it in front of me, even though it tasted shit – they got a kick out of seeing how sick it made me.

Turns out I wasn't as untouchable as I thought. They'd been after me for years. I wasn't stupid enough to think they weren't aware of who I was, but I honestly did think that I had it nailed down so tight, I'd never get caught. They'd sent me some 'mystery shoppers'. They'd gathered Intel from every crook and scumbag going. There were a lot of people that were happy to see me put away. A lot of people. And that included some who I had thought were close to me. Just like my enemies, the Old Bill seemed to have an eternal hatred for me. They'd wanted to get me for some time, and now they had me.

I started to get dressed; I knew those bastards weren't going to give me anything to eat or drink.

'Hurry up, Sommers, The Well has a cell waiting for ya, and I got to pop round your bird's house and give her a good seeing to.' How original.

'You can fucking wait, you pig.'

One of them grabbed me, right on my wound.

'Come on, then!'

'ARGHH!' I screamed.

Before he knew what had hit him, I'd punched him straight in the face. He went crashing to the ground. His mate set about me with his huge stick. I tried to fight back but, once he hit my wound, I fell to the bed in agony. The other plod got to his feet and they both beat me with their sticks. They were cowards. I was a bad man but I was weak, hungry and I'd been shot. In no position to defend myself.

I had been polite to start with. Even though I was this big-time crook, I'd not been arrested before – I had no idea how to conduct myself around the police or anyone of authority. I was naïve, really. I thought that if I was polite and played the game, I'd be treated fairly. But they were brutal. Fair wasn't even in their vocabulary. Sure, I'd been unfair in the way I did things but I knew what I was – a crook, a villain, or whatever you want to call me – and so were the people I did business with. I wasn't a bad man pretending to be a policeman. I didn't take the moral high ground and claim to uphold the law while all the time being as violent as any thug. I wasn't a bully in a silly outfit.

My politeness and attitude did nothing to improve my treatment. They abused me and just saw my politeness as a weakness. They mocked me and ridiculed everything I tried to do or say.

When Casey had taken me on, it was for my ability to hurt people. But, as I got better known and more powerful, just the threat of me was enough. I got my reputation from ten years of intense violence. Violence ran through me; it was my backbone, my makeup. I soon realised that I had to bring that side of me back with the coppers. Fight.

The door to my room sprang open. Obviously the noise we were making had spilled out on to the ward. A nurse burst in. The two sweaty pigs stopped in their tracks, sticks in hands. I was curled on the bed, in a foetal position.

'What the hell is going on? Don't you know this man has recently been shot?' she said, in astonishment.

'Listen, Miss, this piece of shit has just assaulted me. We've had to restrain him.' They put their sticks away.

She gave them dirty looks. She knew I'd received a beating and that they'd probably gone a step too far. One of the coppers had a tooth missing and a bloody nose. It was obvious who'd done that to him.

'Well, I think . . .'

'You think nothing, Miss. You get on your way. We know how to deal with this piece of work.' She left the room, looking uncomfortable and scared. But, in the end, she decided to look the other way, as most would. Cover and arse is what most people are concerned about. Look after number one. She took that option. I don't hold it against her.

'Right, you cunt, hurry up and get your shit together. We're driving you to The Well now and we ain't got all day. Get your arse in gear before I do you some permanent damage.'

I was a potential Cat A since the crimes I was being accused of were high profile, violent and I had links with organised crime – all reasons for why I was being remanded into custody. The Crown Prosecution Service needed time to build a case against me. They chuck you behind the door if they think you are a possible danger to the public or to the case while it's being investigated. If you're found innocent after spending several months, or in some cases years, inside, it's just tough luck. I was hoping to be found innocent but I'd been caught with my pants down. I was hoping that my lawyer would spin some shit to make the book they were going to throw at me a little bit lighter.

I was scared, though. I was about to enter the unknown. A place of vermin and scum – a place where I'd have to pay my tax.

But Donnie? What the fuck happened to Donnie? I daren't ask the two horrible pieces of shit in my room. Did everyone get shot, nicked or did they make it away? All these thoughts were running around my head. I had steam coming out of my ears. And all the fear and danger was making one thing happen. The voices were shouting at me, 'FUCK THEM. KILL THEM. THEY ALL GONNA DO YOU.' Beads of sweat formed on my brow; I opened and clenched my fist. The fire was burning and it wanted to spread. I was evolving into a darker Davey . . .

One of the coppers cuffed me, then cuffed himself to me.

'It goes like this: you do anything other than what you're told to do, I will crack your fucking head. You talk when you've not been spoken to, I will crack your head. You so much as look at me in the wrong way, I will put your lights out for good. Don't think this is some idle threat either. I'm waiting – PRAYING – for you to give me an excuse, you piece of shit. Everyone is skipping through hoops that you're off the street. But there would be even more of a party if you were DEAD. Go on, give me that chance, I dare you?'

I calmly looked ahead.

'I said, GO ON! What you got to look forward to? Rest of your life sucking cock for rock and fucking men?'

'Yeah, he's a fucking iron mate, he'll love it,' the other one goaded.

They were trying to get me to retaliate. The voices in my head screamed. My top lip curled; I was having visions of cutting both their heads off and shitting down their necks. I knew if I made the wrong move, I was proper fucked. I truly believed they would have beaten me to death. When you are a certain level of criminal, it isn't the normal bobbies who deal with you. Oh no. It is a hardened special branch. They are the biggest villains around, but they get away with it because they are supposedly doing it for the sake of justice. Bollocks. Those guys would have taken me out, if I'd have given them half a chance. I knew it. Even the voices in my head knew not to succumb. The door of my room opened. I was going out on to the ward. I'd have to walk the hall of shame.

Most guys who get sent down get taken to prison in the sweat box – a dirty big van with tiny cages to sit in. Because of my profile, though, I was going a different way. The Old Bill had arranged an armed escort – I should have felt honoured.

I stepped out of my room, shackles on, sweat on brow. My heart raced, my breathing was rushed but I saw everything in slow motion and the sounds around me echoed. My dignity was gone. The man of power and control who I had been was lost.

There were a thousand eyes leering at me as I slowly walked though the ward. Each step slower than a tortoise. The two coppers looked at me with a laugh of hatred, revelling in my predicament. Scum, animal, bastard – he deserves it, they were all thinking. I saw the two armed police standing outside the room. They had the look of mercenaries in charge of their weapons. They gave no thought to who I was, or what I was about. They'd been given a duty to guard, and that's what they did. They were a different breed to the two holding me. They wanted to hurt me, to humiliate me.

The ward was full of patients and there were staff buzzing around. In my trance-like state, I felt the atmosphere change. My presence made them feel uncomfortable. Just the armed guards and two coppers that looked like villains would have been enough to make anyone feel uncomfortable.

A thick curtain of scared silence fell. Everyone stopped what they were doing. Stare at the circus act; look at the monster in cuffs. I stared ahead, only interested in the door at the end of the ward. But it was too far to keep my attention. The whispers, the noise of their thoughts screamed at me. Shut up, shut up. 'FUCK THEM, FUCK THEM, FUCK THEM,' a voice screamed in my head. Focus on the door, just a few feet away. The laughs of the pigs hurt. Their voices; the evil in their eyes. The door wasn't far now; concentrate on the door.

My palms got wetter; my forehead dripped. They stared. They watched. 'CUNTS ARE LAUGHING.' No more, shut it, I'm nearly out – the noise in my head was too much . . . 'You want a fucking PICTURE? Who fucks with ME?' I screamed. Release. 'COME ON!'

My frustration echoed round the silent room. I felt a crack to the side of my head, a flashlight of blindness, then I was on my knees.

'Take these off, YOU'RE DEAD,' I screamed, motioning towards the cuffs.

They dragged me across the floor, hurrying me out of the ward. In my blind rage, I saw the looks of relief in the eyes of the patients and staff, as the bad man was removed by heroic law enforcers. They hadn't seen what had come before. They couldn't hear the screams. How could they judge me? But judged I was. Damned.

As I got outside the ward, into the hospital corridor, some more size-twelve hell was unleashed. A nurse came rushing out to us. Between blows, I saw her approach. My saviour; some help, at last.

'Thank you, gentlemen. The patients and staff were all very scared.'

The sporadic kicks and punches continued in her presence. She was PLEASED I was being removed by force. Pleased that I was being served tough justice. That hurt, and I'm not talking about the blows from the pigs. All she saw was a foul-mouthed criminal. A wanted man; a danger to the streets. But the noise in my mind, the starvation and water deprivation, the lack of sleep and the humiliation had started my journey into becoming something even worse. A sick man. Scum. Vile. A closed fist of unreason.

I sat in the car staring into the abyss until it stopped. I looked around at the over-the-top escort I had been given. Over-the-top was an understatement. Sure, I was a good catch and a dangerous man, but they were doing everything they could to make a spectacle of the situation. It was a joke. Them the heroes, me the laughing stock.

I looked out of the window to see a weathered, old, dirty-looking gate, sat between two towers. 'Welcome to The Well, Mr Sommers, I'll just show you to your room . . .' Sinister grins cracked across the faces of those transporting me. They knew something I didn't.

The large gate opened slowly. It was like a fissure appearing in the floor after an earthquake. I'm sure they did it slowly to add effect. It gave you a sinking feeling, like your freedom was about to be beaten out of you.

I felt exhausted. Totally drained. I didn't feel angry, I didn't feel sad. Nothing. Just empty. Tired. This was how I always became after an episode of violence; extreme exhaustion followed. It is a time when I feel a kind of peace. But it's a sad, hard-won peace.

'Wake up, fuck face, you're nearly home.' My zombie appearance and lifeless eyes had been noticed.

I tried to shake some life into myself. The huge door had finally opened enough for the car to drive through and I got my first glimpse of the screws.

We stopped in a sterile area, where the vehicle was searched. It seemed as if even the screws didn't trust the good-for-nothing police.

The coppers got out of the car. There were several screws standing around drinking coffee, chatting. In no rush to start the search. When they felt ready, they began. It got on the tits of the coppers, which made me happy. Maybe it wasn't going to be so bad at The Well?

That hope was short lived.

The screws chatted with one another, not giving a fuck about anyone else. One of them was walking around the car with a mirror, checking underneath. He was laughing and joking with the others. They all seemed to be more human than the pigs. Then he got to the window next to where I was sitting. I looked at him. His laughter stopped. His grin changed into a concrete leer.

'The fuck you looking at?' he said.

I continued to look.

'You keep eyeballing me, lad, I'll poke the fuckers out.'

I turned to face forward. You won't be getting an en suite room here, Mr Sommers.

Once the search was completed, the coppers got back in.

'Looks like you're gonna make a ton of friends here. The screws are very hospitable, as you can see.' They both laughed hard. Comedians.

The gate in front of the vehicle opened, letting us inside the perimeter wall of the jail. I was in. We had to drive round to reception, which was quite a way. No pretty receptionists here or big desks with smiley and helpful staff standing behind them. Reception at The Well was not like that at all.

We drove slowly, past people roaming around. I saw several screws darting about; some looking official, carrying papers, others standing there smoking. So much standing, so much smoking. I saw a group of guys dressed in prison garb. They were carrying bin liners, being escorted by a screw. All smoking. They looked as though they were getting on. They stopped in their tracks to look at the car. They recognised it for what it was.

'Cat A blood, BLUT BLUT!' one of them shouted.

I don't know if he meant it as a respectful welcome, or if he was just pleased to see the mighty fallen.

I looked out the window at the imposing building in front of me. The first thing I thought was, HUGE. Fucking huge. It had windows that went five high and God knows how many wide. Each window had metal bars on it. Some were broken; some had bog roll attached to them. I'm sure I saw shit smeared over a few. Dirty. Filthy. Stinking. That's what I was faced with. The car window was open and once I caught a glimpse of the living quarters, that's when the aroma first hit. One sense activating the other. The sight of the main wing made my nose work in overdrive.

As we continued, we came to a building adjoined to the wing. A bloke came out dressed in a tight vest and blue shorts. That was the first time I saw a gym screw, or PEI. He stopped the car and ushered a small group of cons out of the gym. They came out jogging, and the PEI joined in. I was amazed that this fella was taking a group jogging. As we carried on I looked into the building through the bars, to see several cons lifting weights and other gym screws milling about.

I started to wonder how big the bloody place was. We came to another building, where I saw two well-dressed women coming out. Well dressed and good looking. They were civilian teachers. I was amazed they were allowed to walk around so made up. The coppers leered like pests. So did I!

We came to a stop. I was starting to feel again. I was

pleasantly surprised by what I'd witnessed. A load of guys walking freely, collecting rubbish; a gym that looked relaxed, where you could go jogging out in the open. Pretty girls. The vision was a lot nicer than I was expecting. But visions don't always paint a true picture of what lies beneath. They airbrush reality.

The driver stayed in the car but the two coppers started to get out.

'Get your arse out. MOVE,' one of them barked.

We were outside reception. There were some lads banged up in their cells who yelled down.

'Fucking filth, hope you DIE.'

I smiled at the remark.

'Funny is it, CUNT?' I got a firm dig in the sides.

We walked to the gate. My wrists were killing me. I'd had my hands cuffed together for too long. When they had dragged me off the ward, it had really caned my wrists. I wanted to get inside so I could get them off, which wasn't what I had expected to be feeling when I got to prison.

There was a doorbell and one of the coppers rang it. A minute. Two minutes. Three. They all came and went. Finally the door opened and I was confronted by a fat face, round and grey.

'What?' And a personality to match.

'Sommers, transport from the hospital.'

He took a large swig from his steaming cup and gestured us in.

The coppers removed my shackles. Bliss. I rubbed my wrists hard. Pain relief.

'Arms up,' round face ordered.

'What?' I answered.

'Don't you fucking "What?" me. Mr Stone, or Guv to you. Now lift your fucking arms.' He plonked his cup on the side, spilling some of the hot brew.

He rubbed me down, pressing hard on my body. He came to my wound.

'ARRGGHH!' I screamed, jumping back, bumping into the coppers behind me.

'The fuck you doing?' Mr Stone shouted.

The coppers pushed me forward.

'I was shot,' I said.

'Address me Guv or Mr Stone.'

'Guv, then.'

'Less of the fucking attitude, huh. You a big man, playing with guns then, were ya?' This old sweat didn't take kindly to villains with guns.

'We've had his gob all the way over here and he assaulted us,' one of the coppers piped up.

'I suggest you go get a tea in the office and get out of the fucking way, then.' Mr Stone didn't fuck about. He hated criminals and the police.

They scuttled off.

'So, some gang bigger than yours put a bullet in you?' he enquired.

'You could say that.'

'Who? I need to know in case you could get into bovver here.'

'The Old Bill shot me.'

He held my stare for a few seconds, trying to weigh me up. 'You ain't gonna give me any shit in here, son?' He was experienced. Tough, but fair. He had a way about him that I respected straight away. He was pushing retirement, by all accounts, but was still a firm hand.

'Just gonna do what I gotta do to survive.'

He ushered me further into reception. It was quiet. There was a con milling about, pretending to clean the floor.

'Yes, bruv,' he said as he walked past.

I gave a courtesy nod. I looked to my left to see the screws' office. Fucking loads of them sitting in there. Not enough seats. The coppers were with them laughing and joking, trying to play the 'big I am'. Other than that, there weren't many people around.

The place smelt of a slaughter house. Dirty meat. An unclean butcher's. I could feel the aura of violence and pain, floating in the air. It was intimidating. Fierce. It could crush a man. I was Davey Sommers, the main man. I couldn't – shouldn't – be scared. But I was.

Mr Stone walked round to the other side of the desk.

'I thought this place was a busy nick?' I enquired.

'It is, but all the movement happens in the morning. You with your personal escort have arrived at our quiet time. I don't like being disturbed in the quiet time. That's something you're gonna have to learn.'

Turned out that reception was busy first thing in the morning; getting people out to courts and new arrivals coming in. The evening was busy, with those returning from court and the newly sentenced. But during the day not much happened. And the lazy bastards took it out on anyone who disturbed them.

I was asked a series of questions by Mr Stone; name, address, age, etc.

'Stand over by the wall, in between the two green lines. Face me and don't move.'

He took a photo.

I noticed a screw come rushing out of the office into reception with two others.

'Done?' he asked Mr Stone.

'Yep, take him through.'

'Move,' one of them ordered.

He was less hospitable than Mr Stone.

I was led through to a room which had several cubicles and a desk. The cubicles were all next to each other, facing out.

'Get in there and face me.'

I didn't know what was coming, but I was certain I wasn't going to like it. One of them went behind the desk opposite the cubicles, while the third bloke stood by and watched.

I got into the cubicle. The screw just stared at me.

Eyeballed me. He didn't look happy. He was the biggest of the three. He carried more meat than he should, but looked strong. He was about my age.

'Think it's tough beating up coppers, do ya?'

I refused to answer. The pair of pigs had obviously been spouting off in the office.

'Right, give me your clothes, one item at a time as I ask for it.'

They were taking my stuff to put in storage. I was told what item to give and when. He then passed it to the bloke behind the desk, who marked it down and slung it in a box. They took all of my clothes until I was totally naked. I later found out that they are supposed to hand over the prison kit, allowing you one new piece of clothing as one is taken off. They still get their man searched but allow them some sort of dignity in the process.

'You this big boy, with a button for a dick? You're fuck all, mate,' he said, goading me. 'You think that little flesh wound is something to worry about? You're fucked in here. FUCKED.'

I didn't have the fight in me. The voices were silent. I was able to ignore him.

'Now squat to the floor,' he ordered.

'What?'

'The fuck you talking to? "What" is not how you speak to me, you cunt. Bend your knees and squat to the floor, now.'

They wanted to check I had nothing concealed up my arse. The thought had never occurred to me to do such a thing. How times change.

He threw me a prison tracksuit and pumps to put on. I got dressed as quickly as I could. As I did, the screws in front of me began whispering to each other. All looking at me in turn. I tried to listen to what they were saying, but it was too difficult. They were too far away. I started to feel intimidated again. I was in pain from the earlier fights. I just wanted to keep my head down.

I was dressed and ready, and I stayed in the cubicle, standing to attention. I daren't leave. I knew I was going to have to fight them if I didn't do what I was told. My searcher/intimidator returned.

'Right, you're going to the wing.'

He was standing too close to the cubicle entrance. He was inches away from me. Inches.

'Come on then, shift yourself.'

He didn't give me any room to manoeuvre. He stood right in the doorway.

'I said, fucking move.'

I went to walk past but he didn't let me through, so I stood still again.

'If you don't move, I'll fucking move you.'

I clenched my fist, rubbed my head. What did he want from me? WHAT? Ordered to go, but no room to leave.

I went to squeeze past him. I felt his hand grab the back

of my head. BANG! Before I knew what had happened, I was on the deck, my face down.

'WHAT THE FUCK YOU DOING?' I screamed. 'GET OFF ME.'

The other two dived in. I didn't know what they were doing. They began wrestling with my arms and legs. I thought they were trying to kill me. I managed to boot one of them in the bollocks. He fell back off me, freeing my arm. I then began to leather the bastard who'd dropped me. I punched his face as hard as I could. I didn't have much room to generate power, but it was enough. Enough to knock him back a little.

Then I heard a bell ringing. It was ringing loud.

'FUCKING COME ON!' I screamed. 'YOU WANT ME, YOU GOT ME!'

I wanted nothing more than to get to my cell. Just get out of reception and try to settle in. Try. I could have been the Fairy Godmother and they still would have fought me. They wanted me. They'd been filled with shit from the filth that had brought me in, and they'd decided to serve a bit of retribution. Their provocation hadn't worked so they took the next best option. Engineer a bend up. Stand in the way. Force me to touch them. Give him a reason to start the use of force. Now that they'd started, I wasn't going quietly. Why the fuck should I? They didn't know what I could be like; they got it wrong.

As I heard the alarm, I continued to struggle with the

three who'd bent me up. I don't think they'd bargained for the fight left in me. I'd not bargained for the fight left in me. Adrenaline had kicked in and tiredness had left. Give your wrist to be cuffed, or break the hand that tries.

I heard the sound of heavy feet running towards us. Thank God, they're gonna get these bullying fuckers off me. But I didn't know how things worked. Green to the system.

Several shirts turned up and stood there watching the fight. The alarm had been raised, the troops had run to assist but no extra help was immediately required, so they stood and watched. Occasionally we broke off from our fight, resting like boxers in a huddle. Fight, rest, fight, rest. I saw Mr Stone standing there with a radio in his hand.

'No further assistance required. Senior Officer Stone, out.'

The alarm bell stopped ringing. I was fucked, totally exhausted. They'd finally managed to place cuffs on my wrists and I was face down on the floor.

'What happened?' Stone asked the screw who dropped me.

'He assaulted me when he came out of the cubicle. Shoved me hard in the chest. To prevent any further assault, I placed him under restraint.'

'YOU LYING CUNT!' I screamed.

Although my wrists were in cuffs, they were still using wrist locks to hold me in position. They applied some pressure. It didn't cause me the pain it should have. My hands were numb from the fight. I was numb inside.

Mr Stone told me how to move, to get me to my feet. I was in a standing position, but bent over at the waist. One of the screws had hold of my head; the other two had hold of my wrists in cuffs on my back.

'I'm going to let the officers stand you up fully and let go of your wrists, if you won't fuck about anymore. You gonna behave?'

'Yeah.'

My head was slowly let up. My wrists were released. All I could see were several pairs of black boots huddled around me. As my head came up, the boots turned into trousers, trousers into white shirts. Then I saw the faces. First I noticed were the smiling faces of the coppers standing at the back, loving what had happened. Then the sight of the screw who had hold of my head; the bastard who dropped me. I bit my lip. I clenched my fists.

'All right, son?' Mr Stone said.

I breathed hard. I breathed fast. Lip curled. Pain entered. The smiles. The laughs. FUCK THEM.

'ARGHH!' I screamed and I threw myself into the screw in front of me.

I was smashed to the floor.

'It's the PIGS. FUCKING PIGS. I just want to go home. YOU FUCKERS. COME ON!' I was spouting violent gibberish. I just wanted to be heard. To be seen for what I was. Not the criminal. The man underneath. The mistreatment. The pain. Help. HELP.

I struggled like mad. No water, no food. Bullet hole. Violence. I'll show them. No peace. Hatred, I had plenty. They leant me back, with two screws placing their arms under my armpits and through my legs, lifting me off the ground. It fucking hurt. I was carried bent double, sitting on my cuffed hands behind my back. It was painful. Very painful.

'Hello, tango, tango from SO Stone. Permission to move one inmate under restraint from reception to segregation, over?'

The radio went silent for a few minutes. They had to make sure everyone on the wings was behind a door, so I could be taken through the prison. Stone listened intently at the radio. The order came through.

'Let's move,' he shouted.

I was carried through reception and on to A Wing. My first time inside and I was being cuff carried. It set the tone for me. It set the tone by which I was going to live. I was not going to be broken.

We stepped on to A Wing. There was a huge empty space. Huge. In my agony, I was still overcome by the sheer size of it. I heard bangs as doors closed. The inmates kicked at them to show their acknowledgement. There were officers at their work stations, watching the freak show of Davey Sommers being carried into nick. I was on show. Famous in the prison within minutes.

We walked off the wing and into the centre of the jail. It

was like the body of a spider – each wing being one of its legs. From the body you could see all the way down the legs.

I was taken straight across the centre, to D Wing, which stood opposite A Wing. As we got on there, I noticed a set of stairs that led underground. The Seg. Step by step, they took me down. In there waiting were a handful of screws, all wearing rubber gloves.

I was handed over to them, the Seg screws. They carried me into a cell that had no window, no bed, no sink; in fact, it had no fixtures at all. It had one light that shone a subtle and dirty shade of yellow. They put me down and stood me up.

'You are in the segregation unit. I don't know the reason why you were brought here, and I don't care. What I do care about is how you behave now you are here. I'm going to perform a strip search . . .'

'No cunt is looking at me again! I was only just fucking searched,' I interrupted him.

'It's rules of the block.'

'No fucking chance.'

'You do as you're . . .'

'FUCK YOU!' I screamed.

BANG! I was dropped to the floor once more. They didn't fuck around; they knew what they were doing.

They took the cuffs off and held me on the floor in a figure of four leg lock while they cut my clothes off. Once again, I was naked. They held me down on the floor, then retreated from the cell, like a flash. Before I knew it, they were gone. BANG! The door slammed shut.

I lay on the floor in a broken mess – naked, bruised and battered. My bullet wound was weeping, my body hurting. I was starving hungry and delirious from dehydration. I scrambled to my feet, falling more than once as I did so. I looked at the horrible cell, the brown, dirty walls. A place that had seen more violence than you could imagine. The back of the closed door blended in with the rest of the walls. Side to side I looked, searching for something that would explain how I'd ended up there. I clenched my fist and gritted my teeth. I started beating my chest like a bear on a rampage.

'FUCK YOU!' I screamed.

I fell to my knees in total exhaustion and pain.

'Fuck you,' I spoke once more, no longer having the energy to shout.

My fast breathing began to slow. My sight began to blur. My eyelids shut. The pain eased away. A moment of peace. Emptiness. Just before I drifted off, my last thought and hope was that I wasn't going to wake up . . .

INVADERS MUST DIE

Round and round. Round and round. ROUND AND ROUND. The monotony of day was killing me. I felt like a hamster circling the yard. I couldn't bear the conveyor-belt life.

Guys sat around the side, others performed body weight exercises. I saw smiles, laughter and joking as people got on with it.

Man does what he can to kill bird, but for some it never gets easy. Never. All the years I served behind the door, it was never easy. I always had to work at it. But, for some, it's nothing. What it does to the mental state is worse than the physical. Tenfold. A punch, a kick, even a stabbing hurts, but it's not in the same league as the thought of a punch or a kick; or, more importantly, the fear of one. The reality is never as bad as our brains would have us believe. That's how you survive. Your brain anticipates the danger.

But behind the door, your brain tells your body that your whole life is not nice. Some people can switch off to it and just do the bird. Others battle from the first day until the last. Those who found it easiest were the ones who lacked a certain level of intelligence – level of thought is probably a better way to describe it. They had a one-dimensional approach which put them in good stead when the nights were long and the silence deadly. But I had a constant battle with my thoughts, which made it extremely difficult for me to cope.

As I walked round the yard, I felt very alone. I'd not been on the wing long. Since my infamous arrival at The Well, I'd spent a long time on the Fraggle Wing being treated for severe dehydration, a fractured wrist, two cracked ribs and an infection in the bullet wound.

It was OK over there. There were some complete head cases who didn't know what day of the week it was, but also ordinary blokes who had ended up there for one reason or another. They used to send the extremely violent cons over, those who could only be controlled by medication. But, as bad as all that sounds, I liked it. It felt like a hospital. A lot dirtier and rougher than a normal hospital, but still it had an atmosphere that was different to a normal wing. And that made it feel a little less like prison, which made me feel slightly more free. The time on the Fraggle Wing had sorted me out to some degree. I was still suffering from bouts of anger, something I needed help with but, overall, I wasn't too bad. I was on remand, waiting for trial, so my thoughts were focused on that. Although it wasn't looking good for me, I told myself it was.

While I was on the Fraggle Wing, it got round the nick how I'd been brought in. The fight I'd had and the man I was. There were a lot of people inside who knew me already. A lot that I'd dealt with on the road, one way or another. Being who I was gave me a bit of kudos. But not as much as you'd think. I'd have to earn a rep again. The minute you walk into prison, you're relegated to the bottom of the ladder. You have to prove yourself all over again. Back to basics. Not only that but, because it was my first time in, people wanted to see me crumble. It can happen to the toughest. Plus, there were plenty of people who meant fuck all to me on the road but who were ready to do me inside – it would improve their rep and be putting down a potential new threat on the wing.

I walked around the yard, looking from left to right. There were some faces I recognised, many I didn't. I didn't approach anyone, though. I waited for a signal from them before I spoke. I'd done over so many people, I couldn't remember who was who.

'Got any burn, bruv?' asked Mikey, my new cellmate.

He was one of the fellas I'd done some business with over the years. I had him crack a few heads and push some gear for me. He was a reliable grafter. Loyal. After all the shit he'd done, he ended up inside for having a pissed-up fight with an off-duty copper. Mikey did have a tendency to hit people with whatever he could find – a bottle and the copper's head met. Mikey didn't take kindly to being called a 'fucking nigger'. The copper was just as much at fault but who were the courts going to believe?

He'd done a couple of years so far and was in the know. He knew who to trust and the rules of the game. He was well liked by the other cons. He fucking hated the screws. Hated them. He couldn't understand why anyone would want to work in that shit hole for rubbish money. He didn't get it and, for that reason, he didn't trust them. He said it took a sadistic fucker to want to do it. Even so, he knew how to play the game – smile at them, spit daggers behind their backs.

'Yeah, mate, I got some burn,' I answered, getting out my Golden Virginia.

I'd given him plenty of tobacco since we'd been banged up together. He was taking the piss a bit, but I let him. He had the upper hand. He was more experienced inside and he knew full well that I'd get somewhere in there. That or break. So, while I was in purgatory, he had his few minutes of power. I was happy to let him have it. He was my safety net, the only face I was pleased to see.

'What's happening?' I asked.

'Fuck, man, people are seriously out for you. Bones wants you taken out. He thinks you're gonna get among the dealing and take over.'

'I told you before, I ain't fucking interested. I just wanna do my bird, ya know. Any cunt fucks with me, I'll do them, end of. But I ain't dealing, I can't be arsed.'

And that was the truth. I didn't want to deal drugs inside. It didn't even enter my thoughts. I was struggling too much with my surroundings to have been able to regroup and start up shop. I had a lot of anger inside of me. Hatred of the system. I'd been hurt and didn't want to take any hurt again. From other cons or the screws. I was prepared to fight if I needed to and that was it.

But my reputation wouldn't let me blend in. Everyone expected a certain kind of reaction from me. Perhaps the fact that I was a big-time crook should have meant that I fitted in, but it doesn't necessarily work like that. It does for some. Not me. I felt like an outcast.

'It don't matter what I think. Bones thinks you're here to take shop. He said he ain't having it and you're gone.'

I turned to look at Bones. He was an albino, about six feet tall. A weird-looking bastard. Menacing. He was standing the other side of the yard, dealing. He was blasé about it, too. He had at least two screws bringing in gear for him.

As I looked, he caught my eye. He had a dirty grin on his face. Unclean. I continued to walk.

'Who's that with him?' I asked Mikey.

'Salty. A really horrible cunt. Batters people for fun. The screws are shit fucking scared of him as well. Him and Bones are tight as fuck.'

'Bones, Salty, what is this fucking place?' I laughed as I said it.

'Seriously, bruv, they are fucking horrible. They bully new blokes into stashing their gear. And take out anyone who comes on the wing who might be a threat. It sends out a message. They don't like invaders of their patch.'

I knew that a little chat wasn't going to resolve the situation with those two. As much as I was uncomfortable with prison life, I wasn't a mug. I knew exactly what it was going to take to make them see sense. Make them see what I was about and, more importantly, what I was capable of. I wasn't naïve. I knew what needed to be done.

'MAKE YOUR WAY TO THE DOOR, PLEASE,' one of the screws screamed.

Exercise was over. I walked slowly with Mikey. I weighed up Bones and Salty. They both stared at me, trying to be menacing. They weren't. They aggravated me. Annoyed me. Had just succeeded in winding me up. How dare they think they could fucking hurt me? HOW FUCKING DARE THEY? I started seeing visions of myself hurting them. Cutting them. I saw blood. Screaming. Pain. The burning feeling of hate had started to boil in my stomach. I was focusing now. I wanted to inflict pain on them. 'GO ON GO ON GO ON,' the voice in my head shouted. I clenched my fist. My lip curled. My vision went tunnel, sound echoed.

'Easy, bruv, not here. You fucking mental?' Mikey whispered.

He could see the look in my eye. Feel the tension in my body as we walked.

Salty stared back, miming the words, 'Come on', enticing me to fight.

'Davey, for fuck's sake, listen to me. There're screws everywhere. And there'll be a load of cunts who'll join in.'

SNAP. And back. I managed to regain control. I was on a knife edge. I listened to Mikey. I waited, but stared.

'FOURS!' screamed the screw.

That was the call for me and Mikey to return to our cells. Salty and Bones were left on the yard waiting for the call for the Fives. As I walked through the door, Bones caught my eye. His eyes were a subtle shade of red. He looked almost dead.

I walked through the Ones and saw the screws running around, frantically trying to bang the wing up. Exercise out on the yard, return to your cell, bang up, sowsh and workshops, then lunch. The factory line of prison life.

'What you gonna do?' Mikey asked, as we walked up the stairs.

I didn't answer at first. I was deep in thought. Battling with my mind.

'Davey man, you're fucked!' said one geezer, who was making his way back to his cell.

I ignored him. Concentrated. I had questions thrown at me from loads of blokes. 'What you gonna do? How you gonna do it?' I ignored them all. It was a bit of gossip for everyone else. A fella comes to the nick, fights all the way down to the block, is on the Fraggle Wing for ages, then is brought over to A Wing where he's going to try and overthrow Bones. That was the gossip.

The domino bangs echoed around the wing as the cell doors slammed shut. I got to my cell and stepped inside with Mikey following behind. BANG. The door was closed. We had the usual fifteen minutes before unlock for sowsh. I sat on my bed, staring at the wall. My knee moved up and down at a thousand miles an hour. I knew what I was going to do.

'What cell they in?' I asked Mikey.

'On the Fives, blood.'

'I fucking know that, WHAT NUMBER?' I shouted.

The nerves were starting; the adrenaline pumped. My lips wobbled as I spoke; my shakes looked like a tick. My mind was jumping all over the place. Speaking helped to subdue it a little.

'Eighteen, blood. You OK?'

I stood up and began to pace the cell. Up and down. Round and round.

'Yeah, prepping myself.'

'What you gonna do?'

'What do you fucking think?' I snapped. 'Sorry, Mikey, just getting myself ready. You know how it is.'

'You need me to help, yeah?' Loyal to the end.

It was my fight. It was me they wanted. I didn't want to turn it into a turf war. I wanted to make a fucking statement.

'It's my show, bruv. Tell you what, though, I need a flask. I ain't been given one yet. Can I borrow yours?' As inmates, we were given flasks to collect hot water. There was a huge urn down on the Ones, where you filled up. There weren't kettles in the cells.

He looked at me knowingly.

'Course.'

'Sweet, Mikey.'

I took deep breaths. I went from the window to the door, to the bed and back again. I dropped to the floor and banged out some push-ups.

Before I knew it, I heard the repeated crack of the doors being unlocked. I got to my feet. I grabbed the metal flask. I stood there, staring at the door, waiting for the screw to unlock us. Mikey was standing behind me.

'You sure now's the right time?'

I didn't answer. There was no need. I'd made up my mind. Besides, there's never a right or wrong time to inflict pain. If it has to happen, my philosophy was: get it done.

CLUNCK, CLICK. The door was open. I ran out of the cell like a thousand gazelles. It was sowsh. Some cons stayed in their cells chatting, others came out for showers and phone calls, as and when they pleased. Others roamed the wing. That was the point, it was free time. Doors were unlocked.

I ran downstairs as quickly as I could. I wanted to fill my flask and get up to the Fives, pronto. Nobody seemed to take much notice of me. I got to the urn, pulled the lid off and started to fill the flask. The water trickled out. I willed it to speed up. As I looked round, my hand moved and went under the water.

'FUCK!' It was scalding hot.

The screws were all busy unlocking doors, scratching their arses and drinking brews. There weren't really that many around, though. It wasn't difficult to go about your daily business without them noticing. Besides, not many of them gave a flying fuck what we did. End of the day, all I was doing was filling my flask.

The water had reached the top. I was ready to go. It was heavy. Seriously heavy. Just how I wanted it. I ran up the stairs, by which time there were a few more guys coming out of their cells. I got to the Fives. Mikey had gathered half a dozen or so lads to watch the entertainment. I didn't care. I didn't even acknowledge their presence.

I was on the landing heading to the cell. The place where I would face my foe. Exorcise the demon. 1, 2, 3 – I rushed past the cells – 7, 8, 9 – nearly there. I could see the door. See it had been unlocked. It was only just open. I slowed down to have a recce before my attack. I closed in. I started unscrewing the lid. I felt the steam of the hot water touch the skin on my finger. I was inches away. All I had to do was get in there. Bones appeared on the landing. QUICK.

'OI, CUNT,' I shouted.

He looked at me. I threw the boiling water in his face. He sounded like a pig in a slaughter house, he screamed in so much agony. He fell back into the cell. I followed him, cracking him round the side of the head with the flask. He was on the floor within a second. Salty was having a piss at the time. Before he even looked around, I smashed him over the head with the flask. It wasn't going to be that easy, though. Oh, no. Salty didn't go down. He turned round, swinging a punch at me, catching me on the chin, knocking me back into the wall. I dropped the flask. He got to work on my torso, punching it as hard as he could.

That's when I heard cheering. Mikey and the lads were at the door watching.

I grabbed the nearest thing to me, which was a CD player. I smashed that over his head, which put him on his arse, on top of the blistered Bones. Salty was still sitting upright, though, so I got hold of his hair and started punching his head with everything I had. I then reverted to using my knee, driving it into his face. I heard the sound of a whistle going and I stopped.

'Davey, get out, SCREWS ARE COMING!' Mikey screamed.

I let go of Salty. He fell in a heap. Both of them were smashed up. I had done what I had to do. I showed them – everyone – not to fuck with me. Davey Sommers had taken control. I admired my handiwork – for a few seconds too long.

CRACK! I felt the surging pain rip through my calf, making me drop to one knee. I turned round to see a screw had smashed my leg with his stick. He went to hit me again, but I managed to grab his weapon. That wasn't enough, though. His size-twelve boot kicked into my chest.

'LET GO!' he screamed.

I didn't. He booted me again.

'NOW, YOU CUNT!' he demanded.

That was the first time Mr Cramfield and I met . . .

DARKLY DREAMING DONNIE

The smell of paint was still fresh. Even so, the magnolia still had a dirty tinge to it. But at least it was clean. Ish. Prison was magnolia city. That and dirty snot green, which was the colour of most of the doors. I was down the Seg and the cell I was in was remarkably sterile. The fixtures, which consisted of a bed, sink, toilet and table, were all nailed down tight. They looked newer than most. That along with the fresh paint told me the cell had been refitted and repainted recently, due to some previous damage. A fight. A battle of shirt and con. Or maybe the guy in here before me had shit up? Whatever the reason, the cell was clean. Empty, but clean.

Down the Seg, there are strip cells and Seg cells. Strip cells are what you're taken to when you've been bent up. They are the dirty, empty, windowless, soul-crushing cells. Once there, most guys give up the fight. They know it's over, so they comply. If that happens, you are not in there for very long. You're put into a normal Seg cell. They aren't the Ritz, but they are a damn sight better than a strip cell.

I'd been bent up by Cramfield and his lot and brought down the Seg. Once they got hold of me, I didn't really fight. The odd struggle and kick, but nothing to write home about. I was strip searched, as normal, then put into a Seg cell for the night to await my Governor's adjudication.

The night had been long because it was bloody cold. The cells were too hot or freezing, never comfortable. The window to my cell was broken; the only damage that remained from the former resident. They'd obviously forgotten to fix it. Or, more than likely, they had left it so the next scroat would freeze. I did.

I heard the day staff milling about and the cons starting to wake. I was still cold, so I got on the floor and banged out some press-ups. It got my blood flowing and the energy pumping. It made me feel more alive. My door opened.

'Breakfast's up, Sommers,' the screw said.

He passed me a plastic bowl, spoon and a packet of cocoa pops with long life milk. You didn't get your full English in there.

I finished my cereal and did some more press-ups. I was

sick at looking at the walls. Staring at nothing. No pens or pencils. No reading material. Just magnolia. Lots of it. The more I looked, the closer the walls got. The window shrunk, the bed changed size. Hallucinations flooded my mind when I was left alone for too long without anything to do.

I sat down. Stood up. Walked up, walked down. Press-ups. Walk. Sit. Wank. Anything to kill the bird. I started to think about my time inside. How long was I going to be there? What was I going to do to survive? Donnie – what the fuck had happened to him? My best mate and not a word. Was he dead? Was he in the nick? Fuck knows. I needed to know, though. I wanted to know how it was all going to play out. I was praying for a reduced sentence. My brief was an elusive fucker, though. Wouldn't return my calls or letters. That wasn't a good sign.

The door to my cell opened.

'You're up first, Sommers. Governor's here now. Let's go.'

The Governors took the daily adjudications in the conference room. It was like a mini court hearing. The evidence would be given, the statements read, the con would have a chance to defend themselves, and then the Governor would make their decision. You didn't really stand a chance. The Governors would back their staff. You could say it was all a bit biased.

Occasionally, you got a Governor who broke the mould and would be fair. And sometimes you'd get a totally inept wanker, with less backbone than a jellyfish, who would just adjourn the case or throw it out. They didn't have the bollocks to dish out a punishment, just in case it came back to bite them on the arse. Cowards. But great for the cons.

I stepped out on to the landing and saw Governor Heal. He walked into the adjudication room. Cramfield was standing there, as well. He looked smug, as though he'd caught me bang to rights. I stepped inside. Governor Heal sat behind a huge desk. There was an SO who read the evidence. Cramfield was there to give his evidence himself. There were also two of the biggest block screws known to man, who were standing next to me, just in case I decided to belt some fucker.

After stating my name and number, I was seated. The SO read the charge sheet, stating that I was responsible for the savage assault on Bones and Salty.

'How do you plead?' Heal asked.

'Not guilty, Guv.'

He was making notes of everything.

'Mr Cramfield, if you can tell me what happened, please.'

'On Monday morning, at approximately ten-twenty hours, I was walking along A4 landing when I started to hear a lot of commotion up on the Fives. When I looked up, I saw a large group of prisoners screaming and shouting. It was apparent to me that they were cheering on a fight which was happening inside a cell. I blew my whistle to alert the wing. I shouted the location and ran to attend. As I got there, the prisoners disbursed from the entrance to A5-18. I ran inside to see two inmates had been savagely assaulted and were lying on the floor. Prisoner Sommers was standing over them, breathing heavily. As Sommers is a Pot Cat A, with a history of severe violence, I took no chances and placed him under restraint.'

All true, as it happens.

'Thank you, Mr Cramfield. Sommers, if you can tell me what happened, in your own words.'

'Well, Guv, I also heard the commotion, but I must have been closer than Mr Cramfield here. I ran up to the cell and saw the two lads in there having a scrap. I felt it was my duty to get in there and split them up. You see, all the guys were just cheering them on. I couldn't believe it. I thought someone's gonna get hurt unless they're stopped. So I pushed in to help. But they'd already beat each other half to death, by all accounts. The next thing, I've been bent up by Mr Cramfield here. I don't want to make a complaint, though; I know he was only acting in their best interests.'

Cramfield looked like he was going to explode. 'You lying bastard, it was a fight that was going to . . .'

'MR CRAMFIELD, BE QUIET,' the Governor screamed.

He made prolific notes for a few minutes. Cramfield stared daggers at me.

'Now, what is it you wanted to say?' Heal asked Cramfield.

'Sir, everyone knew what was happening on the wing. We all knew that a fight was about to happen. Something was brewing. It is obvious what happened.'

'Obvious it may be. But, might I suggest, if you have Intel on something, you act on it before that thing happens. I find there to be no evidence to substantiate the charge. For that reason, I find Sommers not guilty. May this be a lesson learned. And, Sommers, you're pissing into the wind at the moment; I suggest you take a long hard look at yourself because, believe me, it will catch up with you one way or another. Thank you, gentlemen, take him away.'

I laughed my head off. The damage I'd done in the fight didn't even get a second thought. I'd got away with it.

I left the office and one of the block screws escorted me back to my cell. Cramfield stayed behind to speak to the Governor. He got a right bollocking. That was the first and last time he nicked me. We were both fairly new to the system. He realised then that nicking me was a waste of time. He decided to deal with things his own way in the future.

I got back to my cell and started thinking deeply about my case, Mum, Dad and Adam. I was more worried about them than me. That sounds clichéd, but it's true. I knew it must have been extremely hard to have a son like me. Doing the things I did. Adam was working as a cardiologist. He was flying. Someone to be proud of. I wasn't jealous. Envious, yes. Jealous, no. I sat there, contemplating my future. Or lack of it. I wanted to know what was going to happen.

My cell door opened.

Cramfield walked in – slowly, staring me straight in the eye. He didn't flinch. I stood up from the bed, staring back. I clenched my fist. He was there to dish out some retribution. He wasn't going to bend over and take it up the arse from a scroat like me. Step by step, he edged closer, not taking his eyes off me for a split second. He wanted to let me know he wasn't scared of me. Show me that he was also a man behind that uniform. It was working. He wasn't afraid. Wasn't intimidated. His walk, his look – everything about how he conducted himself spoke a thousand words.

He got within a few inches of me. Nose to nose. We stood at a similar height. Similar size. Two men from different sides of the fence. Neither of us took our eyes off the other. We were sending out a message to each other. We both knew, in that instance, that we were going to be the thorn in each other's side. We'd said our piece without saying anything at all. Words weren't needed. We knew.

'You've got a legal visit. Let's go.'

He led me to the legal visits area. It was like an office block with several individual interview rooms. You're given a room to yourself, so you can speak freely. I never felt it was totally free, though. I always thought that the screws and God-knows-who-else had learned things about me that I'd only ever said in there.

Cramfield left me with the officers who worked visits. I was shown into one of the rooms and seated. My lawyer was at the main gate. Once I was located in the visits area, he was brought over.

I sat there looking around at my new surroundings. Observing. Always observing. My new life was a far cry from the life I used to lead – nice cars, good clothes. And women. I was a philanderer, all right. I took full advantage. I like sex with women. Being in The Well prevented any of that. The sexual frustration was a killer. It may sound minor but, if you're into sex, being starved of it is particularly harsh.

The door to my room opened. In walked my lawyer, George. A very tall man with a huge, curly mop of grey hair that was overgrown and needed a cut. Although it was thick, he had a perfect circle of bald patch on his crown. And a big face. Very long. He had a striking resemblance to Jeremy Clarkson. He was also a no-bullshit type of person.

I stood up and shook his hand. Firm. I like that. Can always tell a lot about the character of a man from his handshake.

'Why have you not been taking my calls?'

'I've been extremely busy, David. I've several cases I've got to deal with so it's a waste of my time waffling crap to you, when I've got nothing concrete to say.'

Fair point.

'I've been stuck in this shit hole, going out of my fucking mind, George. I need to know what's going on.'

'You need to try and keep your head down. I've heard all sorts about what's been going on in here. It's not good for your profile when you get to court. Not good at all.' He'd made a career out of dealing with guys like me. He wasn't there to massage my ego or give me any sympathy. That wasn't his job.

'OK. What's happening then? When am I getting out of this fucking place?'

'David, look, you know that you're going to do a fair bit of time here. You know that. I've not tried to hide it.'

'Yeah, but you said you might be able to get some stuff thrown out. Get a lower sentence or something. I don't know, do your fucking thing. Do whatever it is I pay you for.' I was getting anxious. Scared.

'I will do "my thing" but I'm not a bloody magician. I work with what evidence I'm presented with. I've now got yours and it's not looking good.'

'What does that mean?'

'The prosecution have got a top witness. A fucking whistle blower of some kind.' He started to look at his notes.

'Who? There ain't no one that's got fuck all to stick on me, 'part from the coppers who nicked me that day,' I said, through broken laughs. Nervous. Thinking. It couldn't be.

'Ah, let me see . . . Smith. Donnie Smith. He's given you up, so it would seem. The whole lot. Appears he's been working as an informant for some time.'

My world came crashing down. Donnie. My mate. My ally. The only guy I'd ever trusted had sold me out. No wonder I'd heard sweet FA from him.

George went on to tell me that the only things left at the lock up when the police went to search it were 'my' firearms and pills. Donnie had given them fucking everything. EVERYTHING. My whole network.

The games I'd played in my head, kidding myself that I might, JUST MIGHT walk at the trial, evaporated right there. There was no hiding from it now. I was caught, bang to rights. Not only that, they had a star witness to nail me with. I could no longer pretend I was going to get out. All of a sudden it was very real. I was going to get life in prison. It was just a matter of how many years . . .

A TALE OF A CHEMICAL ROMANCE

My hands were like ice. White and bloodless. I rubbed them hard against each other. I pulled at each finger, urging some heat to return. The shirt under my suit was damp. No, soaked. My skin was leaking. I looked down at my front and it was as if I'd had a bucket of water slung over me. Cold. Clammy. Uncomfortable. I was breathing too fast but I couldn't taste any air. My chest tightened.

As I looked around the courtroom, the silence was deafening. I looked at Mum and Dad; they were holding each other's hands tightly. Adam gave me a wink and a brotherly thumbs up.

This was it. The sentencing. After a long and drawn-out

trial, I was found guilty of possession of firearms, causing ABH on a police officer (that bullying piece of shit at the hospital) and the big one – obtaining money by intimidation.

George had done well by me. With a combination of discrediting some evidence and negotiating with the prosecution, he'd managed to get the drugs charge thrown out, among other things. I had even been up on a kidnap charge because I'd forced that buyer back to his flat. Even though what I ended up being accused of wasn't as bad as it could have been, the obtaining money by intimidation charge could bring a lot of years with it, or so George told me.

It was now my day of judgment. I feared the worst, but hoped for a bit of undeserved divine intervention.

I looked at George, who gave me a nod of recognition. I looked at Mum, Dad, Adam and back at George again. I stared at the judge, then down at my hands. I wished that fucking old poof would get on with it. HURRY.

'Mr Sommers, I've had the opportunity now to consider the appropriate punishment for the crimes you have committed. All of the evidence that's been given to the court suggests to me that you are an extremely violent and dangerous man. It's apparent you have an appetite for leading a life that is not, by any means, acceptable in today's society. You have no respect for those people who come up against you and will do anything, no matter how heinous, to achieve your ultimate goal of gaining control, power and money within the underworld. When you have had the opportunity to speak, you have made it clear that you see nothing wrong with your actions; that they are a natural hazard of "people in your line of work". You are a very naïve man, Mr Sommers, to think that your criminal activities and your network of violence only have repercussions within the criminal world. In my eyes, you have been a very fortunate man to have had a number of the charges discounted. And I wholeheartedly believe that this has been due to a flaw in the legal system and not due to your innocence. You are a very dangerous man, one that I can no longer have walking the streets. You have shown no remorse and are an embodiment of hate. You are a threat and a danger to peaceful society. I find no alternative than to sentence you to life imprisonment, with a minimum tariff of fifteen years.'

And there it was. Fifteen years. The room fell silent. Horribly silent. There were no tearful screams from Mum. I didn't threaten the judge. It wasn't how I'd imagined it would be. It was very clinical. I expected something more. Much more than this silence. Here was a decision that changed the rest of my life. It was the death of my freedom. A man like me had changed the course of my life with those simple words; someone who had lived and learned but who had just chosen a different path, a lawful one, had changed everything. I couldn't help feeling that there something was wrong. It was wrong that my life could be taken away based on the decision of just another man.

But I'd spent my life doing the same thing – making choices for people, taking things from them, changing their lives and sometimes ending them. I'd played judge for years. But when the judge gave me my sentence, I didn't see it that way. I thought he was mental. I was caught up in my own misconception. I wanted freedom but I didn't deserve it.

I was a prisoner long before I was arrested. Long before. The judge took away my physical liberty, but it was the start of me. It was the best thing that could have happened. But it was going to get a lot worse first.

The court screw came and got me, and started to take me down to a cell. I walked slowly, looking around the room. It was sombre. No matter who the villain is, when a life sentence is dished out, it creates an atmosphere in the courtroom. Everyone imagines themselves in the same position. Everyone thinks, 'Thank God that's not me.' And, 'His life is finished.' With that comes a feeling of sorrow – not for the convicted but for themselves. Emotions are running high and the sadness and sorrow in the room can be felt so strongly, it's almost physical. The people who worked in the court and those in the spectators' gallery had their heads bowed. It was strange. I expected tears or abuse. But got nothing. Just this sadness and that made it even worse, even harder to bear. I would have welcomed screams of hate. Something.

I looked up at Mum, Dad and Adam. They looked down

at me. Tight lipped but trying to give half smiles of support. They were pained. Out of their comfort zone, as I was. The reality of what my sentence meant was hard to take in – I wouldn't share a meal, or go for a walk, or watch TV with my family for at least fifteen years. The sentence had been handed to my family as well as me. I felt like I'd been cheated.

The memory of my sentencing brings so much pain and upset. It was extremely hard. I was overwhelmed by fear.

I sat in the holding room underneath the court. It was cold and dirty. I could feel the hate that filled the room. The fights that had gone on in there; the pain felt by men served life. The melancholy and sadness I felt was soon replaced with anger. Ferocious anger. That fucking bastard Donnie. How could he? How could he do this to me? After all the things I'd done for him over the years. The money I'd given him, the friendship I'd shown him. All repaid by being royally stabbed in the back.

But was I a true friend . . . ? I told him what to do. I never let him make any decisions. The family and kids he had were an afterthought for me. So long as he did what the fuck he was told, all of the time, I was happy.

I may have been in charge but, make no mistake, Donnie was also a wrong 'un. He loved the criminal life. He loved the money that came with it. The kudos and lifestyle. The power. That's what his driving force was. That and my knuckle duster. But as he got older and got himself a partner and kids, he wanted more from life. And I wouldn't allow it. No way. He was my right-hand man and I needed him.

He may have grown sick of the criminal life but it was too late; he'd made the choice to be a part of it and you can't escape once you're in. It's not as if he could just hand in his notice with me, then fill in an application form to work for the Post Office. How can you explain away twelve years of unemployment without claiming a bean in benefits?

I had my legit businesses but Donnie had fuck all. I wouldn't let him. I was jealous. Although I was the boss and I had the money and I decided how it was going to be, I didn't have the love of a good woman and I didn't have children. I didn't have that closeness. He had a whole other existence. I had nothing but the Firm. Yeah, I had girls. Shit loads of them. A fuck is a fuck, as crass as that may sound. Sexual gratification is one thing, closeness is another. I always had the former, but didn't have a clue how to achieve the latter.

Donnie wanted to provide more for his family so I gave him wads of cash. He didn't go without. But he wanted more; he wanted a sense of achievement. A sense that he was moving up in the world. He wanted to 'stand on his own two feet'. I didn't listen. And, frankly, I didn't give a shit. I just wanted him to do what he was told. Like most of my relationships in the past, it was a one-way street.

Turning to the Old Bill was his way out. His way to a

better life. It was the only way open to him. Two children, a wife and a life of crime. Like I said, I wasn't going to give him his P45, a good luck card and a handshake. Nor was he going to head down to the job centre. He chose the only way out that he could.

But that afternoon, sitting in the cell under the court, I didn't see it like that. Oh, no. He was a dirty, good-for-nothing grass, and if I ever got my hands on him, I'd fucking kill him. KILL HIM.

I started to pace up and down the cell, thinking of Donnie. Visualising him in a nice witness protection house. Smiling. Laughing. Enjoying his new freedom. He'd cost me mine. There was no other way I could see it. The visions of his happiness haunted me. I wanted to destroy him; kill him. I'll find him, I'll find him. Fuck him, if he thinks he's getting away with doing this to me.

The coldness in the cell evaporated. The heat of rage had started to flow. Then the realisation of my fifteen-year sentence came flooding back. FIFTEEN YEARS. I'd managed my time on remand by picturing freedom soon. I'd convinced myself that George would wave his magic wand and get me out of there. I would lie to myself, pretending I could walk away from it all once the trial was over. Convinced myself that the time I'd served on remand would be enough; that I'd get probation, community service, something like that. That was my bird killer.

What the fuck was I going to do now? Thoughts raced

through my mind. Fear. That dream of freedom, however much it was pretence, was my way of getting through it all. That and fighting the system. It gave me purpose. A reason to live. Dreams of freedom and fighting were my ways of dealing with it. Now it seemed that fighting was going to be the only way to live behind the door.

Truth had dawned. I was to be a prisoner for fifteen years. How was I going to cope? I marched up and down that cell. Back and forth. Back and forth. BACK AND FORTH. To fight. TO FIGHT. That's all I had left.

I crouched down, lifted my trouser leg up and reached deep into my sock. I pulled out the spliff I'd been carrying. Since I'd been on remand, apart from imagining my freedom and fighting the system, weed had become the third way I killed the bird. Smoking copious amounts of it. I didn't touch anything harder. Just weed. I wasn't one of them dirty bastards that took the scummy drugs. I wasn't a junkie. Not yet, anyway. So many convicts turn to chemical bliss when they are served a severe sentence. Some people arrive inside already hardened drug addicts, but for others it blocks everything out once they get there. Helps you cope. A man behind the door will do anything that helps him cope. When I'd been caught, I saw users as dirty junkies. It was OK for me to sell drugs, it was even OK for me to take them occasionally, but become addicted or take the 'wrong' kind of drug and you were dirty. Pot, kettle and black.

The spliff was squashed and bent from being inside my

sock for so long. I did my best to straighten it out. I didn't have a lighter, though. You weren't allowed one in court. You also weren't allowed to smoke in the court cells. During the trial I'd managed to sneak one in, occasionally – sometimes it resulted in me being bent up at the end of the day but it was worth it. A career hazard of the smoking prisoner.

Now I had a spliff, but no lighter. Chinese torture.

'Guv, GUV?' I shouted, as I kicked the door.

There was no other choice. There was one screw on duty to look after all the guys banged up in the court holding cells.

'GUV, GUV, can ya come here a second, please?' I kept banging. Kept pleading.

The spy flap in the cell door opened.

'What is it, Sommers?' the guard said. A grey-haired, tired-looking man. Probably an ex-copper.

'Is there any chance I can have a light, for this?' I showed him the spliff, hoping he'd assume it was a rollie.

'You know there's no smoking in here.'

'Please, Guv, I'm begging you. I've just been given a fifteen. I'm going out of my fucking mind in here.'

He looked at the ground, then back up at me. He did this two or three times. I heard the keys jangle, the handle snap into position, the heavy door opened. YES. He took out his lighter and struck the flame. I put the spliff into my mouth. I saw him screw his face up when he saw the size of what I was smoking. He knew what it was. He wasn't stupid. But what could he do to me that was any worse than a fifteen-year stretch? Nothing. He could have taken it away. I had nothing to lose by trying. NOTHING.

I stuck the end of the spliff into the flame. I puffed hard until it was lit. The sweet, sickly smell and taste flooded the cell, and wrapped around the guard in front of me. He coughed. I smiled with a little light relief.

'Sit at the back of the cell and don't leave fuck all of that in here, OK?'

'I won't, Guv, I swear. I just needed it, you know? Fifteen years. That's a lot for me to swallow. I need it today.'

He nodded. 'I know, son. But don't leave fuck all of it in here. It's more than my job's worth, understand?'

'Sweet, Guv. You're a diamond.'

The door slammed shut. I sat on the floor at the back of the cell, like he had told me to. I sucked hard on the spliff, wanting it to end the pain and fear. On each toke, I was convinced it was doing just that. As I got more stoned, I felt a little more relaxed. For a while the pain and the worry disappeared. But it didn't last long. Weed wasn't having the effect on me that it used to anymore.

My knees were sore from the continual knocking. Sitting in the sweat box was cramped for the smallest of men. And I wasn't the smallest of men. My elbows banged on each side, my torso slumped over at my waist. My arse cheeks were dead numb. I fidgeted to relieve the pain but there was no room to move.

I looked out of the smoked windows. Getting inside The Well's perimeter wall was pleasing for one reason and one reason alone: I would be able to stretch my fucking legs. As I looked out the window, up at the big wing, I felt different. Different to when I'd arrived here before. Uneasy. Sick. Every time I'd seen it before, I had the hope of escape. This time, though, I knew it was going to be my home for the foreseeable.

We crept round the final bend and came to a stop. We'd arrived at reception. It was time to go inside and not come out again. For years. I'd always had the trial to focus on. Legal reasons for leaving the prison – not that they were days out that would give you bundles of fantastic memories. It was an uncomfortable ride in a shitty van, then into a cold, dark cell under the court, followed by hours of scrutiny from some tit in a wig. But it was a day out. A day away from the conveyor belt of life in The Well.

The door to my tiny sweat box opened. I stood up, feeling a rush of pins and needles flurry down my legs. I was numb and cramped.

'Today, Sommers.'

Moody fucking bastard. I was going as quickly as I could. Physically I was tired but mentally I knew it was the last time I would be entering reception in a long time. The last time I would be wearing my suit, or any of my own clothes.

The last time I would look up at the sky on the other side of the fence. It was hard. I had a lump in my throat. I felt tears in my eyes, I'm not ashamed to admit it.

Memories of Sunday roasts with my family, Christmas Day, walking in the park, sitting in a pub garden, swimming in the sea, going on an aeroplane, driving in my car, sleeping in my own bed, walking to the shops, going to restaurants, cooking for myself, going to the cinema, playing squash, wearing aftershave, using decent toilet paper, sunbathing, sitting on a sofa, late-night trips to the supermarket, going to bed when I wanted to, holding my mum, listening to my dad, laughing with Adam, eating when I wanted to, karaoke, kissing, sex, love, smiles, money, home, freedom, FREEDOM, FREEDOM, FREEDOM . . . My head was going to explode.

I got out of my box and edged down the walkway, off the van. I had a sudden rush of claustrophobia. I felt squashed. Like I couldn't breathe. I wanted to be in the open. Breathe the fresh air.

I looked up at the sky this side of the wall. Then I looked around, taking in the surroundings. The huge wall covered in barbed wire. The screws darting around in their unsightly uniforms. The bars. The searches. The struggle with boredom. I stood there taking one last deep breath. One last look up at the sky. I knew I had to head inside. Head back to jail. The sentence had been given. The time had to be served.

I walked in the gates and was faced with Mr Stone.

'Arms up, lad,' he said, in a calming way.

He was respectful to me. He could obviously see the anguish on my face. My body language and awkwardness said a thousand words. Men who have had their liberty taken away were something Mr Stone had seen a million times before. He knew how a prisoner must feel.

He rubbed me down, half-heartedly. I don't think he wanted to be anal about procedures; not with me on that day.

'How did you get on?' he asked.

'Fifteen, Guv.'

When I said that, the lump in my throat came once more. I could feel my eyes beginning to fill. Saying it out loud made it even more real, if that was possible. More and more real. It wasn't getting easier, but more intense. Fuck. FUCK.

There was a slight bow to Mr Stone's head. A respectful recognition of my predicament.

'You'll do it standing on your head, son,' he tried to make light of it.

I couldn't even force a smile. A few tears trickled down my cheek. I couldn't speak.

'Head down, go with the flow. That's what you need to do. Trust me; it'll be easier that way. They'll leave you alone.'

'They? Who the fuck is "they"?' I wiped the tears away. 'You're one of them, so don't fucking make out you're any different.'

His advice – his GOOD advice – was thrown back in his face.

'I'm a dinosaur, an old sweat or whatever you wanna call me, and, yeah, I'm a screw, to state the obvious but I've been round the block here, Sommers, and I think I act like a fairly decent man. I've got my faults but I don't do to others what I wouldn't expect to have done to me. Because of that, I can give advice to anyone – a screw, con or the little, green fucking man. And my advice to you, son, is keep your nut down. Go with the flow, otherwise there'll be people who will take great pleasure in breaking you. Great fucking pleasure. Do whatever you want with my advice, but I suggest you take it, cos if you don't you won't make another fifteen months in here, let alone fifteen years.'

I wasn't ready to listen to advice. I wasn't even close. I was closed off to who I really was. I was in my own little box, and my ego began to shout. Fucking SCREAM at me.

As I walked across the landing, back to my cell, I looked down at my prison garb. I'd just had my clothes bagged and tagged. This was it. My uniform for life.

The wing was fairly quiet. Everyone was behind their doors, except the servery workers down on the Ones preparing dinner. A screw unlocked my cell door and walked me in.

'Yes, bruv,' said Mikey.

'All right, mate,' I answered.

'Well?'

'Fifteen.'

'Nah, bruv, that's fucking harsh. HARSH.'

He went silent. Mikey rolled up a fat joint and passed it to me. I slumped on my bed and sucked the life out of it. I wanted something to numb me. Take away the pressure.

I looked around the cell – the dirty sink, shitty walls, the broken toilet, the wafer-thin mattress. The stink. STINK. I looked up at Mikey. A friend now, a real close pal, but the thought of having to live my life in a cage with another man was too much.

I coughed as I ragged the spliff. I couldn't get it down quickly enough. It wasn't strong enough, though. I needed something stronger.

'Ya know what, I don't think I can take this.' I stood up.

'Davey look, you know what you need to do to kill the bird. Get into that mindset. You know you have to.'

'I was. The trial. All that was my focus. My bird killer. But that's bollocks, look where it got me, huh?'

'Don't give me that. That weren't the only thing you did, was it?'

He was talking about the fight in me. The anarchy against the system. I sat back down on my bed. Anger could be my only salvation. It was a way of saving myself from facing the truth.

'You know Tommo?' Mikey asked.

'Yeah, seems like a good lad.'

'A good lad who serves up. Have a chat; he'll sort you out a bit of proper gear. It'll help.'

I just listened, not answering. Maybe some brown would take away the pain. I'd seen the junkies walking around, happy as fucking Larry. They didn't seem to give a fuck what went on around them.

The familiar sound of the doors being cracked open started to echo round the wing. Dinner was up.

Mikey and I walked out on to the landing to the familiar sight of several cons dragging their heels, talking gangster.

'DOWNSTAIRS!' screamed Cramfield, trying to usher us along.

The system was to walk down the stairs at one end of the wing, collect your food from the servery and go back up the stairs at the other end of the wing. So you're always walking in the same direction. Factory line.

I looked round at Cramfield. He had a sinister grin slapped across his fat face. He knew I'd been sentenced that day and seemed to be loving every second of it.

'Hear you're gonna be with us for quite some time, hey, Sommers?'

'I gotta be here. What's your reason, you FAT PRICK?' Fuck him and his pathetic comments.

His smile dropped as the lads on the landing began to laugh. I was out of striking range, so he didn't engage in a fight but I'd made him look like a fool and that wouldn't go without repercussions.

'Let's get downstairs, Davey,' Mikey said, hurrying me away.

I stared at Cramfield as I went past. I think I started to smile a little. It was the first time I'd felt anything that resembled happiness or satisfaction since being sentenced.

As we walked down the stairs, we saw Tommo up ahead.

'Tommo?' Mikey shouted.

He stopped in his tracks, turned and smiled.

'Yes, Mikey, what's up?' They touched fists.

'You know Davey here?' He gestured to me.

'Who don't know Davey Sommers? Fucking bad man!' he said, giggling. 'Don't fuck with him!'

I was only half looking and listening.

'Can you sort him out some brown?'

He stared at me. 'Can you not ask for yourself, bruv?'

I screwed up my face. I didn't take kindly to anyone trying to talk to me without respect.

'I can help you if you want me to, man, I'm here!' He could see my displeasure at his previous tones.

'Yeah, be sweet if you can sort me out. What do you want for it?'

'We can work something out.' He put his hand on my shoulder. 'Come to my cell when you got ya scram.'

I got to the Ones and joined the queue. I felt everyone staring at me. They all knew I was up for sentencing and that it wasn't going to be a short term either. 'What ya get, bruv?' 'What's ya tariff, Davey?' 'How you gonna ride it?' That's all I was getting. Question after question. Most of them were sincere but it was the last thing I wanted to talk about. I was all over the place.

I got inside the servery. The lads serving were all cons, dressed in white, employed to dish out the grub. There were two screws in there as well.

'What do ya want, Davey?'

'Curry and rice, bruv.'

He slopped it on my plastic plate. Plenty of it, too. It was nearly dripping over the edge. I moved along, collecting some bread and a breakfast pack, for the morning. Mikey was just behind me. Tommo had already made it back to his cell.

I slowly walked back up the stairs, listening to the shouts of the other prisoners. The noise. The screams. The dirt. I got to Tommo's cell. I was barely inside, when he gave me two large wraps.

'Take it easy on this; it's strong. Not the normal prison shit. It's my Percy.'

'Cheers, son. As I said, how do you want me to pay for this?'

'Davey, you get my back and we're sweet, OK?'

'Nice one; goes without saying.'

He wanted some muscle. And I wanted drugs. An easy transaction. I walked back to my cell; Mikey came in a few seconds later.

'You get it?' he asked.

I gave him the two wraps. Just as I'd passed them over, Cramfield walked in.

'You, fuck off out,' he ordered Mikey.

'What, where?' Mikey was nervous. I had an idea what was coming.

'I don't care. OUT.' Mikey put his dinner down and went back on to the landing.

Cramfield was sweating with rage. He had hate in his eyes.

'Who the fuck do you think you are, huh? Call me a fat prick, will you? I'll fucking show you. Good job they gave you fifteen years, you degenerate, lowlife piece of shit.'

He walked towards me.

'FUCK YOU, CUNT,' I screamed, throwing my plate full of dinner at him.

His crisp white shirt was dripping with curry. He stumbled forward.

BANG! I belted him hard in the face and then smashed him in the ribs. He managed to head-butt me, knocking me backwards. Blow for blow, we went at each other. I'd have the upper hand, and then he would. Toe to toe we fought, practically smashing the cell to pieces in the process. I managed to crash him to the ground.

'Fifteen fucking years I got today. And you STILL won't leave off. FUCK YOU!'

I started kicking and stamping on him. Mikey came running in. He'd been outside, listening and watching.

'EASY, DAVEY!' He grabbed me from behind, pulling me off. I tried to get back to Cramfield. 'ENOUGH!' he shouted.

I was out of breath, with a bloodied face. Cramfield was on the floor, soaked with my dinner. Beaten. I'd got the upper hand. I'd fought and won. Mikey helped him to his feet.

'You OK?' Mikey asked him.

'Yeah, piss off,' he answered, shrugging him off.

He looked at me. We both stared at each other. There was a mutual respect there. We both realised how tough the other was. We also knew that it was going to be the first of many altercations. He rubbed his body, clearly in pain. He limped out of the cell.

'I take it you're gonna fucking nick me, now? Fucking screws!' I shouted after him.

He turned back and said, 'Cos that worked, didn't it? One nil, Sommers.'

He walked out. He never nicked me for it. He wanted to deal with things himself. He came, he lost, he left. For that, I respected him. I hated him, but I respected him . . .

I had the empty biro in my mouth, sucking hard as I followed the burning fumes of heroin. Mikey had shared his dinner with me and then we'd waited for the count to be done and quiet time to follow.

I coughed and spluttered a little. Nausea followed for a very short time. Then the blanket of bliss started to cuddle me. I slumped back on to my bed. The voice of anger started to quieten. The pain of my situation lessened. My perception of the world around me changed. It became beautiful. I felt warm, content and loved. I felt love. Warm, tingly and comfortable. Heroin. The answer I was looking for. It was everything I thought I needed . . .

IF THE DEVIL EXISTS

'**L**isten, cunt, you had it, you fucking pay.'

'Davey, please, I will have it, just give me a couple of days.'

'Couple of days you ain't got. You got two choices. You sort the money out or, you see that urn over there?' he looked and nodded, 'I'll put your fucking head under it until all your skin has left your face. You understand?'

Debt collecting was easy for me. Fucking easy. There was nothing to it. Especially now I had so much anger in me. It was my purpose. My job. Tommo dealt drugs and I smashed people that didn't pay. I smashed other people that tried to deal. To be honest, I smashed anyone I felt like smashing. I

totally terrorised the wing. It was my release. And my way
of paying for all the drugs I wanted. Heroin calmed me.
Crack was my lunacy juice. Together, they were a cocktail of
destruction.

People say they don't give a fuck but I REALLY didn't give
a fuck. I would have done anything to anyone.

'I can get some stuff brought in. Anything. My missus is
coming up the day after tomorrow; she's bringing the baby. I
can have his nappy loaded up to the max?'

He was prepared to get his partner to fill their child's
nappy with drugs to pay for his habit. Using kids wasn't
uncommon. Low-life junkies would do anything to get a fix.

'You got two days. Two days or you're fucked.'

'Thanks, Davey, I really appreciate it.'

'Fuck off, you mug.' I couldn't stand arse kissers. No
bollocks.

He continued walking around the yard. I looked over at
Tommo, who was brazenly dealing drugs to anyone who
approached him. I watched his back, making sure he could
get on with business without any trouble. Everyone knew I
had his back, so they left him alone.

The screws didn't seem to give a shit. A lot of them
wouldn't recognise a drug deal even if it happened right in
front of them, though. Sure, there were the hawks that didn't
miss anything, the streetwise screws, but there weren't that
many of them. And, a lot of the time, they turned a blind eye
if it meant the wing was calm and under control. Even if the

control was being provided by the wing's drug dealers.

I was taking heroin and crack on a daily basis. I was well and truly hooked. It dulled the shouts of the night, relaxed the mind and made the bird a little easier to bear. That was until the clucks set in. Sometimes, not often mind, Tommo would have a dry period without much stuff. Either the bent screw who brought the drugs in was off, or the exchange in visits had been caught. When that happened, I was in a world of shit. I felt like tearing off my own skin and running away from it. The touch of clothes, the feel of the air; everything felt like punches and pulls. My whole body would become one huge sensitive zone and everything hurt it. The walls would drip. I'd talk to people that weren't there; the sights, visions and pain would all be too much for me. But taking the drugs gave me a temporary release and high. My mind was anything but stable – I'd use the drugs and I'd fight. With anyone. ANYONE – screws, good or bad, other cons, good or bad. Tommo and Mikey were my only friends. I was a part of Tommo's enterprise. He used me for what I was good at and he gave me what I required but I did like to think that we were also friends. I still craved decent human contact. I could have had it. A lot of it. People who are banged up together can become friends for life. Closer than family. Being behind the door with someone for twenty-three hours a day, you will most likely build a close relationship with them.

As much as I wanted to have this kind of closeness,

though, it made me feel more imprisoned. It reminded me too much of my life and relationships on the road. And that, for me, was a killer. I couldn't get through the time if I had friendships that reminded me of the physically free Davey. By rebelling and being a bully, I was giving myself extra survival techniques. Going against the grain and making my own rules satisfied me. Or so I thought. In fact, it just drove me deeper and deeper into myself. Crazy war screams haunted my mind. I was unwell. The crack and smack only added to my lunacy.

'Davey. DAVEY!' screamed Mikey. He'd come out on the yard. I smiled as I saw him running up to me. 'Mate, it's come through, they're letting me out on licence! I'm out of here today!'

I felt a lump in my throat. I was happy for him. No, that's a lie. I was gutted. GUTTED. His friendship was one of the only things that kept me going. I'd spent a lot of time with him, behind the door. Talked a lot of bollocks, taken a lot of drugs. As much as the monotony of prison killed me, life behind the door, life with my pad mate Mikey, was how I liked it; I didn't want it to change.

Probation had been fucking him around tenfold. He could go, then he couldn't. He could stay at his girlfriend's, then he couldn't. He was fit for release, then he wasn't. He'd tangoed with them for months. I never really believed he was going to get out. Well, it was what I used to tell myself, to stop myself from having to face the truth.

'Nice one, son, pleased for ya.' I started to walk off.

Mikey stood there dumbfounded. He wanted to put his arm around me; wanted some emotion at least. Something. I was a hated man. Loathed. But he was close to me. He truly was. He knew that. He thought I'd at least show him something. That I cared. But I couldn't allow myself.

'The fuck's your problem, bruv?' he shouted at me as I walked away.

I just kept walking.

'Davey, I'm talking to you!' he grabbed my arm.

'Get your fucking hands off me,' I said as I shrugged him off.

He couldn't believe it.

'FUCK YOU THEN,' he barked. He began to walk back inside. 'You're one sad cunt!' he shouted.

I just carried on walking. I was sad. Lonely. Scared. I didn't know what was going to happen to me. How life was going to be. The nights. The days. My drug-addled mind didn't mask the sadness. I looked at the ground as I walked. I shouldn't have been so nasty. Why is he able to leave and not me? FUCK. FUCK. FUCK.

'Ah, the missus walking out on you, is she?'

I looked up to see Cramfield on the stairs, on yard duty. He was smiling. Revelling in my misery.

'Fuck you,' I said, giving him the finger.

'Mmm, that's good, Sommers. Let's see how you like it now that we're going to move you down to the Ones to keep a closer eye on you. No more drugs, no more FUCK ALL for you.'

'You think I'm moving, you better get your fucking army, cos I won't be walking anywhere.'

'It'll be my pleasure.'

I walked on. Not only was I losing Mikey but they were going to move me to the Ones. Not without a fight, though.

'Tommo, I need some more gear.'

'You sort that thing out?'

'Course I did, he's getting a load brought in for you, the day after tomorrow.' His face lit up.

'What do you need – white or brown?'

'White. I'm gonna have a fucking tear up.'

I slammed the door to our cell shut. Mikey looked round at me as he packed.

'The fuck you doing?'

I got some paper to block the spy hole. I turned the bed over and began smashing everything up, creating a barricade.

'BRUV, FUCK'S SAKE, I'M LEAVING TODAY. STOP!'

I wasn't listening, I was in overdrive. Anger, hate, fight. My survival mode for dealing with change. Dealing with Mikey leaving. Cramfield had given me reason, not that I needed one, but he had given me a reason to fight.

I knew Mikey would be packing. I knew he'd still be in the cell when I returned from exercise. But I had decided to keep him with me for just a little while longer. It would make the scenario more hard hitting. More noticeable. Those bastards would hear me now. They'd know Davey Sommers only does what he wants.

I grabbed all the butter, sauces and liquids we had in there and put them to one side before I totally wrecked the place. I was breathing heavily. Out of breath. Sweating. Anxious. I pulled off my top. I looked round to Mikey, who stared at me angrily before half smiling.

'You're fucking mental, Davey!'

We both laughed.

'Them cunts want me to move cells. Fuck them! They want me to move, let them fucking move me!'

There was a knock on the cell door.

'OK, Sommers, remove the paper, so I can see inside,' Cramfield ordered

'Fuck you, you useless cunt!'

'Your arse mine, Sommers. I'm coming in with a team and, believe me, YOU WILL FUCKING MOVE.'

'Yeah? Well I got someone with me!'

I looked at Mikey, who was shaking his head.

'Who?'

'Mikey. You come in here, there's gonna be blood and it ain't gonna be mine.'

'Have it your way.' Cramfield walked off.

I jumped around the cell, feeling a little bit more alive. More in control. The voices were screaming victory. The more damage I caused, the more alive I felt.

I pulled out my crack and grabbed my pipe. Suck, breathe, bliss. Suck, breathe, bliss. BLISS. HIGH. FIGHT.

'You're fucked, mate, they're gonna throw the book at you, saying I'm ya hostage.'

'Didn't say I had a hostage, didn't say it was gonna be your blood, did I?'

I was so smug. Thought I knew it all. But what a fall from grace. I'd become a drug dealer's muscle. A drug addict. A junkie. Scum. Lowlife. Hurt, angry and frightened.

It wasn't the prison's fault that I'd become what I'd become, but they certainly hadn't done anything to help. Or to rehabilitate me. I was considered a lost cause. And a fucking barmy one at that. But they should have tried to help an ill man.

'OK, Mr Sommers, I've come to ask you exactly what it is you want from all this? Find out if there is any way we can somehow rectify this situation, without anyone getting hurt.' Someone had started to talk to me through the door.

'Oooh, Mr Sommers, now, is it? What happened to junkie, scumbag or cunt, huh?'

'Errr, well, there's, mmm . . .'

'Errr, mmm, what? You fucking mug! What rank are you?'

'Well, that, erm, doesn't really, mmm . . .' A hostage negotiator at their worst.

'Why don't you take your stuttering self back to the canteen, because you ain't got a fucking clue? I don't talk to anyone unless they're in charge. Get me the Governor. No, actually, get me the Home Secretary. That cunt needs to be told a few home truths.'

Mikey and I began to laugh quietly.

'But, Mr Sommers, I need to . . .'

'I ain't listening, so fuck off.'

Every time someone asked to speak to Mikey, I told them they were there to speak to me and no one else. Mikey sat quietly. Looking at his watch over and over. Watching me smoke more crack while we sat in there together.

Imagine having your release confirmed, after God knows how many years inside, and your pad mate gets you caught up in the middle of a barricade? I'd want to kill me. But Mikey had the patience of a saint.

As much I was the big man on the wing, he knew a different side to me. He knew that I was bad at coping. I struggled with every aspect of prison life. He saw the frustrations, the mental damage I'd suffered every day I'd been there. The fighting was a mask. Some wither and die but my fight was my way out. So I was labelled a maniac. I suppose I was one but, the truth of the matter was, I wasn't strong enough for prison. That's why I was the way I was. Mikey knew that. He knew that the barricade was my way of dealing with him leaving. In a weird way, he knew it was my way of showing I cared.

'Look, Davey, do what ya gotta do, blood. I know better than most we all do whatever it takes to survive.' He put his arm on my shoulder. 'But I think you're gonna have to try another way to ride this. You can't keep this fight up forever, ya know.' I looked down at his hand on my arm. I felt sad. Lost. I put my hand on his and clenched it tight. 'We're like brothers, yeah? I'll come to see ya. I'll be on the other side when you get out. Anything, you need, I'm here.'

We put our arms around each other. We embraced tight.

'Sommers, I'm giving you a direct order, TAKE DOWN THE OBSTRUCTION SO I CAN SEE IN AND GO STAND AT THE BACK OF THE CELL.'

I knew that I only had seconds to play with. Negotiations were over. I let go of Mikey and got back into fight mode. I stripped down to my bare arse. Everything, underwear included. I started to open the butter, as quick as I could, smearing it all over my arms, hands and body. I did this to make it hard for the screws to get hold of me. I'd been bent up hundreds of times, so I knew exactly how they'd do it; I wanted to make it as difficult as I could for them.

'Give me a fucking hand then, don't just watch!' I said to Mikey.

He grabbed some butter and smeared it over my legs.

'THIS IS YOUR LAST CHANCE, SOMMERS. I'M GIVING YOU A DIRECT ORDER – TAKE DOWN THE OBSTRUC-TION SO I CAN SEE IN AND GO STAND AT THE BACK OF THE CELL.'

I started to jog up and down on the spot, charging myself up. I was ready to fight. My lip curled, fist clenched. I smeared the rest of the butter, ketchup and chilli sauce all over the floor in front of me. I wasn't going to make it easy for them.

Mikey cowered down low in the corner at the back of the cell. I was just in front of him.

I heard the door begin to creak after a series of bolts, bangs and pulls. I saw the door starting to open the wrong way. A cell door normally opens inwards. In a barricade situation, they open it the other way. I started to punch my chest. I frowned. I hated. I was listening to the voices in my head, 'KILL THEM. KILL THEM. KILL THEM.' I raged at the voices. I was ready to fight. Ready to maim and hurt. Fucking authority. Who are they to do this? I do what the fuck I want. I'm Davey Sommers.

'I'M DAVEY SOMMERS, YOU HEAR, CUNTS? COME ON!'

My body was tingling. The adrenaline was pumping. The apex of my crack high was reached. I could have smashed down a fucking concrete wall. I could have dodged a bullet, lifted a house, fly. The madness. The noise. The screams.

The door was fully opened. I could see a group of screws behind it, all wearing their riot kit. The first one had a shield. They had to get through my barricade first. They pulled, kicked and punched the broken furniture and twisted-up bed out of their way.

'COME ON!' I cried.

I was salivating. Bursting. I was hitting myself. I was up

for it. MAD FOR IT. They were inches away from getting through the barricade. Inches away from getting to me.

'YOU WANT IT, YOU GOT IT.'

They smashed the last of the debris away and got back into formation. The front guy held his shield with two screws behind. They moved towards me quickly, the screw on the shield lost his footing. BANG. I punched him hard, knocking him to the ground. The slime on the floor had worked. The two others ran around their floored friend and tried to get hold of me. I slipped and slid out of their reach. Each time they tried to get me in a wrist lock, I managed to get away. I punched, kneed. I bit. The screw that had fallen over joined in. The three of them managed to bundle me to the floor but were still unable to get a hold of me. They tried to push on pressure points, scream orders. Nothing. I was a man who felt no pain. A man on crack.

One of them put his finger hard on my top lip, just under my nose, trying to get me to comply. He had thick leather gloves on, but I still managed to get that finger in my mouth. I bit down hard. I didn't pierce through the glove, but I did lock it down tight, like a bulldog.

'He's got my finger. MY FINGER!'

He released his grip from me and lifted the visor on his helmet. The other two had slipped off my arms. BANG! I smashed him in the face. I fought off the other two and got to my feet. I saw a white-shirted Senior Officer at the door who couldn't believe I'd managed to get the better of three screws in full riot kit. I had blood on my mind. I ran to the door.

'FUCK THEM. HIT THEM. ARGH!' I charged hard and fast, leaving the three in my wake.

CRACK. Before I'd got to the door, I was met with the bottom end of a riot shield – the thin bit, like a fucking knife. It smashed me right on the nose. I'd run into it at full pace. The contact knocked me off my feet. I'd been close-lined to my back. I was instantly in agony. I felt like a bucket of water had been thrown over me but it was my blood pissing out my nose that was only just still attached to my face. The blade end of that shield had taken me clean out.

In stepped another three-man team in full riot kit. The fight was far from over. I punched, kicked, hit and fought, using every ounce of my energy. The team I'd evaded in the first place joined in again. They were doing everything they could to control me but it was proving impossible. They tried to get the cuffs on me, but I was two oiled and strong for them to be able to get my hands together for long enough. They tried to pick me up, but I would just hurt one of them, and then I'd be dropped. One by one, the staff fell like flies.

Drug, anger and torment fuelled, the body can do things that you'd never think were possible. Extreme strength and inhuman acts can be achieved when the wayward mind has control. And it had control of me. Strong, fit and mad as I was, the body does eventually tire, though. It took them over an hour to get me out on the landing. One hour and three hospitalised screws. I had a broken foot, a fractured wrist, four broken fingers and an obliterated nose. They put me in a body belt – a belt that has cuffs on each side for your wrists. They are only used for severely mad bastards. That's what was required to get hold of me. All because I was ill. Self-inflicted maybe but I was ill. A man with a mind that had all but gone.

I lay naked in the strip cell, my arms still in the body belt. I was covered in my own piss and shit. The walls were close to me. Too close. I'd been in there for hours. HOURS. The injuries I carried needed treating. I needed relief from the withdrawal I was suffering. I was on a fifteen-minute watch, to make sure I was OK. But I was far from that. When they did check, I screamed at them. Wanting to fight. I wasn't in any sort of control. I was a savage. An animal. But I was disturbed. And I needed help. But I was left to rot in that cell. If the devil exists, he was in there with me . . .

THE JAB, THE SHIELD, THE VISIT

'**S**TAND AT THE BACK OF THE CELL.'

I was sitting on my bed, slowly getting dressed. I was single bang up. I wasn't allowed to have a cellmate. The order being shouted at me was one I'd grown accustomed to. I wasn't fazed by it.

'I SAID, STAND AT TH . . .'

'You can see I'm getting fucking dressed, you STUPID CUNT,' I shouted back.

I took my time. I wasn't in any rush. Make them wait. I slowly pulled on my jogging bottoms, followed by my sweat top and pumps. I'd been sleeping heavily. Very fucking heavily.

I'd been back over the Hospital Wing for some time. They didn't know what to do with me. I was down the Seg at first. But I was a drain on resources, apparently. The staff down there couldn't cope with me as well as all the other refractory Seg dwellers.

I don't remember my time there that clearly. It was one big fight. I wouldn't talk to anyone. Didn't want to. They were all out to fucking get me, I thought. I'd sunk into a hallucinogenic world of utter disturbance. I didn't know what I was doing. I was fraggling out from the withdrawal of my daily heroin and crack. I couldn't cope, plus I was carrying some pretty severe injuries that hadn't been treated.

Every time my door was opened, I'd fight. Every time. That's not the behaviour of a man in control of himself. But the more I fought, the less they wanted to open my door. The more abuse I screamed, the less communication I was given. If someone is nasty or dangerous, you don't want to deal with that person. It's human nature. Even if it was their job, the screws are only human; most of them. They don't want to have shit thrown at them, food slung at them, verbal and physical abuse. That I can understand. But I was left there for far too long. FAR TOO LONG.

I was moved into three different cells. I went on dirty protest. Nowhere seemed too low for me to go. There was no bottom to The Well. The whole time I was there, I wasn't alone. I was speaking to the voice in my head. Being told what to do. It was the worst it had ever been. It drove me.

Eventually, they decided to relocate me to the Hospital Wing. Of course, I wasn't going to go quietly. All I knew was how to be full of violence.

They came in, kitted up, smashing me to the floor. I was jabbed up with liquid kosh that totally took me out. I was a dribbling wreck who couldn't even say his own name. The fight fell out of me. The voices went silent. Numbness flowed through me. It was a break for my body. The fight had to stop some time.

They carried me over to the Hospital Wing and I was put into a single cell. I don't remember how long I slept for, but it was days as opposed to hours.

It was then that I first took methadone. The methadone didn't stop the cravings for heroin. Not for me. Some people it may well do, but it was just another hit to me. I found it good. It was a drug, so I welcomed it. But, not for a second did it make me stop wanting heroin.

The wing was run by hospital screws, who were supposed to be trained nurses, as well. I don't know how trained they were. I think putting on a tunic was as much training as they got. There were also some civvy nurses and a lot of doctors. Although I was there on meds, was I happy? Was I compliant? Hell, no.

Occasionally, I'd play some pool or relax a little. That would be just after my meds. But it wouldn't last for long. I'd soon want to fight, hurt and maim. Being slung in a cell, dosed up to the nines, wasn't the answer. It wasn't the treatment I needed. I'd not even spoken to anyone. No one took the time to talk to me. Yeah, I was abusive, angry and violent, but I was unwell. If people don't like to deal with problems and concerns like that, they shouldn't be in the job.

There was one lady, an officer, who did take the time to talk to me, though. Who did make me feel a little bit more human, though the voices still screamed in my mind. Miss Rogers. She was nice, strong, angelic. She would command authority, but through kindness. She made me feel good. She seemed to care. She REALLY did care. It was more than a job to her. She was the sort of person who had the right balance. She would help as much as she could – really help – but was never a pushover. You took the piss; she let you know about it. Not with an iron fist but she had a way about her that made you feel low and down; that you'd disappointed her. It went a long way with a lot of lads. Don't get me wrong: if she needed to, she would take you down the disciplinary route and, for a woman, she'd get stuck in if she had to. I know – I'd felt it! But, nine times out of ten, her unique style and way of dealing with things was enough to get the job done extremely effectively.

My behaviour was still outrageously bad, by all accounts. I was a danger to those around me – staff and other cons. I wasn't allowed to associate with the other prisoners. I was considered too dangerous. The only time I was let out of my cell was when there were two teams of four screws, in full kit with two shields surrounding me. That's how bad it got.

'HURRY UP, SOMMERS, OR YOU'RE NOT COMING OUT TODAY.' The order was given for a last time. I wanted to get out; had to.

'OK, OK, I'm ready.' I walked to the back of my cell.

I stood there, with my back against the wall, as I did every day. I was fairly relaxed. Something I didn't feel that often.

'SHOW ME YOUR HANDS.'

I waved at them, half taking the piss. The cell door opened and I was faced with a doorway full of shield and screws in riot kit, barking their orders at me.

'KEEP YOUR HANDS IN FRONT OF YOU AND WALK TOWARDS ME SLOWLY.'

I took each step with a controlled and slow pace. I had to. Any sudden movements would result in the door being slammed shut and me not being able to get out for the rest of the day.

As it stood, I was the first out on the wing. On my own for exercise and meds. If that went without any fuss, I might, just might, get a shower later in the day. That would consist of me being walked to the shower by eight screws, being locked in there for a wash and then the eight of them would escort me back to my cell.

That's what I had to look forward to. I got fed at my door. It was too much hassle for them to get me out on my own, walk me to the servery and then back again.

As I got to the cell door, the screw with the shield moved

back, just enough so I could get out. As he moved back, he linked shields with another guy, making a shield wall. Behind each shield stood three men and a further two behind the pack – Good morning, Mr Sommers, sleep well?

The wing was empty, except for the staff who were running around trying to look busy. And, of course, my personal riot squad. I walked to the med hatch.

I always had to move slowly. These screws had been briefed about me. They'd been told that if I made any sudden movements, I was to be smashed to the floor and placed under restraint. Sometimes, there would be a newish officer who hadn't dealt with me before. Fear is a funny thing. More than once I'd found myself bent up and thrown back in my cell, even when I'd done nothing wrong. An over-zealous and scared screw would pounce. It wasn't because they wanted to bully me. Well, not all the time. It would be out of pure fear. Fear that I might go off. And they didn't want that. They'd heard the horror stories. Seen the wake of my destruction.

I got to the med hatch and they passed me my large beaker of methadone. I gulped it down in one. Next to it were a couple of pills and a small cup of water. They went straight down my neck. I turned round to see the wall of shields. I knew where I was going next, but I never moved without checking.

'On the yard?' I asked. It could have been bad weather, or they might have bent me up for deciding to think for myself.

'Yep. Way you go, Sommers.'

I walked slowly out the door. There was a distinct chill in the air. There was a lean-to structure that created some shade as soon as you stepped out. The hairs on my arms stood to attention and a shiver ran down my spine. The yard was up a small set of stairs. I looked up to see the sunshine smashing down on all corners of the yard. It was a beautiful spring morning. Staring at the sky, for a few minutes I felt free. I was so eager to get up those stairs and feel the warmth of the sun.

I started to rush up the stairs.

'Easy, Sommers, the yard ain't going anywhere.'

Step by step, I walked up. Still in the shade. Still in the cold. I breathed the fresh air, deep into my lungs. I had my mouth wide open. I could taste it. YES. I walked through the gate and into the sun. YES. The warmth. The openness. YES.

The gate was locked behind me. I didn't even look back. I didn't care. This was the one and only time each day that I had a sense of freedom. A quiet time. Quiet from the screaming in my mind. It still tried to control me. But out there in the open, somehow I was able not to listen.

I walked round a couple of times, soaking up the atmosphere. It felt like my own place. I was the only one out there. It is a strange place, prison. My feelings, likes and loathings changed over time. Something I liked or needed at one point would turn out to be something I loathed further down my sentence. The evolution of the serving prisoner.

There is no rule book. What it's like for one is totally different for another. What keeps one man sane can drive another to an asylum.

After walking round a couple of times, I did my normal exercise routine. I ran round the yard five times, then did twenty press-ups. Five times, then did twenty burpees. Five times, then twenty sit-ups. I did this continually, until I could do no more. Until I was lying in an exhausted heap. Normally I'd be able to keep it up for about forty minutes. Once I'd had a five- or ten-minute rest, I'd be taken back inside. The other lads on the Fraggle Wing got about half hour. I normally had an hour. As I didn't get out as often as the other prisoners and when I was there I just exercised myself into oblivion, they allowed it.

I sat at the side of the yard, exhausted. I didn't recognise that exercise was something that made me feel better. Made me feel able to step away from the screams. It was something I'd recognise in the future.

The sun belted down on my sweaty brow. I felt my muscles burning from the rigorous workout. I breathed heavily. Felt relaxed.

'Morning, Davey. Did you have a good workout? Looks as though you did!' Miss Rogers greeted me, standing on the other side of the yard bars.

'Morning, Miss. Yeah, had a good one today. Feel good. It's beautiful weather. I could sit here all day.'

'You know if I could let you, I would!'

'Ha, ha, sweet, Miss. What can I do for ya?' I was wondering why she'd made her way out to speak to me.

'There are some people here to see you, Davey.'

'Tell the Old Bill, I got fuck all else to tell them.' I'd had the police come in from time to time, to question me about my crime network and associates. Even though I'd been inside for quite a few years, they'd still show up. And I'd still tell them to fuck off.

'No, Davey, I think you're getting the wrong end of the stick.'

'Miss, they always bother me and it gets on my tits. I got fuck all else to say to them.'

'Davey, it's not the police who've come to see you.'

'Who then, Miss?'

'It's your father and brother.'

My hair was unkempt and still wet. I'd washed myself cleaner than I had in years. I'd not seen Mum, Dad or Adam since the day I was sentenced. I'd refused. I couldn't. It would break my heart. Ruin me. Seeing them would have made it worse.

I'd received several letters from all my family. Dad would write to me every week, without fail. From time to time, Mum would add her own personal note at the end. And Adam would write occasionally, too. They had known what I was before I'd been banged up. In my fucked-up sense of right and wrong, I thought that being a gangland boss was somehow more palatable to them than me being a junkie. I wasn't prepared to show my new self to them. In reality, the boss I used to be was just as bad, if not worse, than the crazed lunatic I'd become. It's just I didn't turn up in a BMW, wearing an Armani suit and smelling of Cool Water anymore. I'd turned into the end product of my old business. The junkie. Just deserts. Karmic law.

As I walked to the visits, I was still surrounded by eight screws but they were wearing their usual uniforms, rather than the riot kit. They were showing my family respect by doing that and saving me a bit of the indignity of it all. Don't get me wrong, turning up with eight screws surrounding you isn't the best way to be delivered to your visitors, but it is a damn sight better than having them in full riot kit.

Miss Rogers had organised everything. My dad had contacted the unit; he was desperate to see me, and Miss Rogers happened to be the one who took his call.

My behaviour wasn't showing any signs of improving, since being on the Hospital Wing. I was more controlled, perhaps – so long as they had eight men and a shield surrounding me and gave me enough medication to subdue a crazy horse – but I was just being contained. It was a drain on resources and if I didn't start showing signs of improvement, eight-man unlock was going to be my reality for the rest of my sentence. My mind would have been blasted into obscurity. Passed back and forth between the prison service and mental asylums. Controlled, but not helped.

Miss Rogers didn't want me to go that way. Although I hadn't seen them, I would talk to her at great lengths about my family and how much they meant to me. I'd tell her anecdotes and she would see glimpses of humanity in me. She was the only one I spoke to like this.

I'd not requested a visit. I was still adamant that it wasn't right for my family to see me this way. But still Dad's letters came. The dedication he showed me was unbelievable. Sometimes I couldn't bring myself to read them but, when I did, his words were wise and full of love. He never gave up on me. Never faltered in his duty as a father.

Miss Rogers had arranged the visit off her own back. Having taken the call, she listened to my dad's request. She told him my current situation. She told Dad I needed help. That if I didn't snap out of the pit I was in, I was screwed, well and truly. She took a risk. I could have said no. I could have refused to see him. I had too much respect for Miss Rogers, though, and what she was trying to do for me.

Also, the fact that Dad and Adam were actually there was HUGE for me. Knowing they were in the same building was too much to bear. I was sick with excitement. Scared with nerves.

As I made my way to see them, we walked through underground corridors and parts of the jail I never knew existed. I wasn't heading to the visits hall, after all. I wasn't allowed to go there. It had been arranged for me to have my visit in the Seg. The good thing about that was I'd be alone in a room with just my family.

I was breathing heavily.

'It will be fine, Davey, don't worry.' Miss Rogers was so kind.

'Do I look OK?' I fiddled with my hair, tucked in my top.

'You look great!'

I laughed. I definitely didn't look great.

As the final gate was opened, I looked down the long, cold landing. The ceiling was so low, my head wasn't far from the top. I saw a couple of the Seg screws standing there, drinking brews. They looked at me differently. They almost bowed their heads in recognition of the nervous and emotional state I was in. I saw the closed door to the adjudication room, at the other end of the landing. That's where my visit was going to take place.

Butterflies flapped in my stomach. Sadness made my arms go limp. I felt weak and scared. I walked on in the centre of a circle of men. I didn't want Dad and Adam to see me like this. Too late – we were at the door. Miss Rogers knocked and opened it. I couldn't see in. The shirt-covered, thick shoulders surrounding me obstructed my view.

'Davey is here now, gentlemen.' Was she speaking to my family? Was she?

The screws at the front filtered into the room and I followed. Move. MOVE. I CAN'T SEE . . .

Adam and Dad stood there, waiting. Smiling. My knees, my hands, my lips – they all shook. My heart was broken. Dad was greyer than before. Not just his hair. He was grey, through and through. He looked heavy with emotion. A man filled with worry. I saw his eyes fill. Adam stood next to him, smiling, playing the fun, big brother. The chubby smile didn't hide his emotions, though.

A choking sound came out of my mouth.

I took the next steps quickly, almost knocking my minders flying. Dad, Adam and I met. We threw our arms around each other. The three of us began to weep. We didn't say anything, just stood there and wept for some minutes.

The screws left the room, leaving the door open. They had every right to stay inside, but they left out of decency. We finally broke our embrace. Dad put his hand on my face, stroking my cheek.

'You've put some weight on, mate!' I said to Adam, joking.

'All paid for, son!' He rubbed his belly.

The three of us laughed.

We sat down at the table, catching our breath. We stared at each other for a few minutes, unable to speak. We were weighing up each other's appearance. We'd all changed – dramatically – over the years.

Dad looked barely alive. The greyness. His skin, his eyes, his hair. Even the sound of his voice carried a grey, awkward pain in it. Had I done that? I couldn't take my eyes off him.

Adam. Fat. Smiley. A doctor. A father. Different. I'd

missed so much of the changing family. I felt like I'd had so much taken away. But it was all my own doing. I felt detached. Unworthy of the Sommers name, let alone their company. I looked at the desk, the walls, the floor. I rubbed my legs, pulled at my hand. How different my life had become. Why had I chosen this path? WHY? I could have lived a good life. Had the kids, the Ford, the job, the semi-detached, Glade plug-ins and summer barbeques. Kids and wife. Happiness.

But, no. I chose something else. People complain of a life of anonymity, the boredom of mediocrity, the daily grind of job, paying the bills, one holiday a year, raising the kids, takeaways on a Saturday night, cooking dinner, milky tea, chocolate digestives, telling the kids off for making a mess. But, I realised as I looked at my brother and father, a life like that really is one of God's gifts.

'David, have you received the letters I sent?'

'Yes, Dad. They give me my mail. Most of it, anyway. I get some letters from people telling me what a scumbag I am and, most of the time, they keep those away from me!' Making fun of myself was my way of trying to deal with the embarrassment of my family seeing me this way.

'Why didn't you write back? David, I've been sick with worry. No phone calls, no letters, no visits? I would phone in, though, did they tell you?'

'Yeah, sometimes.'

'At least that's something. It was the only way I could find out anything about you. Most of the time the officers had very little to say. And, if they did, it wasn't always complimentary, I can tell you that. It made me sad to hear them talk about you like that. It made me sadder that you, my son, wouldn't even talk to me.' He said it all so calmly. Like he always did. No anger.

'Dad, I . . .' I was struggling.

'What?' he said.

'I . . . Just . . . Well . . . I . . .' Fuck, I couldn't get the words out.

'Don't care, is that it?' My Dad was rattled.

'No, of course I care. It's just, I . . .'

'What, Davey? A letter, a phone call – something. You've been taking the piss.' Adam said it how it was. Dad didn't tell him to mind his language, for a change.

'I CAN'T COPE!' I screamed. 'There you go. The BIG Davey Sommers. The crook, the gangland boss, the one at the top, can't fucking cope in prison. And to know I'm going to be in here for years has broken me.'

It was the first time I'd said it out loud. All of the hours in that cell with Mikey and I never actually said it. He knew, but I hadn't said it. Five minutes with my family and boom. Difficult, yet liberating. Cured? Not by a long shot.

'It hasn't broken you, son. Nearly, but you're still here. Alive and well.'

'Wouldn't say well, Dad, he's seen better days!' Adam lightened the mood.

We spoke at length about the regime, the food, the cells, the other cons, the screws. They fired lots of questions at me. I answered them as calmly as I could. I had become an expert on the place. I found myself actually beginning to talk with pride about my knowledge of prison. Sad. Very sad, that I could have sunk to such a level.

'Miss Rogers is a very nice lady, isn't she?' Dad asked.

'Yeah, the best.'

'She has told me all about your behaviour. Your drug taking. Why?'

'Dad, I don't need to spell it out. It's a coping thing.'

'What about the violence? Why do you need eight big men to babysit you?'

I looked to the floor, too embarrassed to answer.

'Cos he's a menace, Dad!' Adam relieved the tension in the room.

'Tell you what, mate, you sure don't act like a doctor. What's up with ya?'

'Cardiologist, actually.'

'You should know better than anyone, then.'

'What's that?' He looked at me confused.

'The benefits of exercise, you fat bastard!' We both laughed. Dad wasn't amused, though.

'David, I've prayed for you.'

I shuffled in my seat. I wasn't ready to hear his religious mumbo jumbo. I wasn't ready to look into the face of God. That was the last place I thought I'd find sanctity.

'I need more than that to help me.'

Dad just looked at me with sadness. He took in my appearance and what I'd become. My sunken eyes and slurred words. My blotchy skin and involuntary twitches. My messy hair and dirty clothes. The smell of dampness and dirt that surrounded me. I'd washed, but I wasn't clean. Even while I was with them, my concentration wandered. I would mutter to myself. The words weren't recognisable, just incoherent mumbles, but they saw it. Saw me trying to quieten the voices in my head.

Dad placed his hands on mine.

'My son, please do as your keepers tell you to do. I can't bear to see you like this. My son,' he said, welling up, squeezing my hand tighter, 'my son, my son, my son.'

I squeezed his hand back. I tried to console him, as did Adam. We talked about the outside world. Adam's marriage and two wonderful children were well. The pictures he showed me proved that. Then the conversation took on a distinctly more serious tone.

'Mum ain't been well, mate.'

Shit, Mum, I'd not even asked about her. I couldn't believe it. I was so overwhelmed to see Dad and Adam in front of me, I didn't think of anything else.

'Where is she? Why didn't she come?'

Dad sat back in his chair with his fist in his mouth, unable to speak.

'Well, she can't, mate. She'd been suffering from

hypertension and she hadn't tried to get help for it. This caused a haemorrhage in the . . .'

'Adam speak fucking English will you.'

He took a deep breath and rubbed his face.

'She always spoke about you, Davey. There wasn't a day that went by that she didn't.' Dad was crying now. 'She would talk about you, like you were still there. With pride.'

'What are you saying?' I was confused.

'Davey, there's no easy way to tell you this . . .' Adam's voice had changed. It was a doctor's voice. 'Mum had a stroke. She passed away at the end of last week.'

The pressure of the room closed in on me. Came down on my head. Suffocating. SUFFOCATING. Help. PLEASE HELP. Adam grabbed my arm. I looked down, confused. We sat in silence. I was hypnotised. Unsure. Hurt.

'Miss Rogers, take me back to my cell. TAKE ME BACK TO MY FUCKING CELL,' I screamed.

My minders came running in. Their faces showed they were ready to fight but I was placid. A zombie. I got up and started to walk out of the room.

'I will be in touch. I love you, mate,' Adam said, as I walked out. He didn't try to stop me.

'God bless you, David,' was all my Dad could muster.

We began the long walk back to the Fraggle Wing.

'You OK, Davey?' asked Miss Rogers.

'You fucking knew, didn't you?' I asked.

'It wasn't for me to tell you. It was for your family. I

thought you deserved that. It could help you, you know? Help to get your life into some perspective. And get yourself ready for the funeral.'

'I ain't going nowhere. You fucking knew. I trusted you.'

'I am here for you. I just . . .'

'DON'T TALK TO ME,' I snapped.

I sat in my cell starring into space. I was unable to feel. I couldn't take in what I'd been told. I didn't know what to do. I wanted to feel something. Hate. Anger. Sadness. But an overwhelming numbness surrounded me. Why? WHY?

I started pacing up and down, punching my chest, slapping my face. Feel. FEEL. Memories of Mum cooking, holding my hand, watching me in the school play, kissing my head, tucking me in, taking me shopping, smiling at me, listening to Dad, telling me off, wiping away my tears, looking at me, fixing my clothes, doing her hair, holding me, making it right, loving me, giving me presents, her smile, her face, her smell. HER SMILE. HER FACE. HER SMELL. Over and over. OVER AND OVER . . .

There was the sound of the cell door opening. I heard the noise but the memories were still with me. I looked round to see Miss Rogers standing in the doorway with my dinner. A plate filled with food. Behind her there was the handful of men required for safety. I walked over to her slowly. She said nothing, just looked on with caring eyes. I reached her and was about to collect my dinner. HER SMILE. HER FACE.

HER SMELL. I collapsed at her feet. Crying. Screaming with pain. The images of Mum were there. In me. With me. I fell to her feet. Screaming louder than I ever had. Miss Rogers knelt down, putting her arms around me. The screws looked on, without an ounce of aggression. I was overcome. Mum. My dearest Mum had died. I'd not had the chance to say goodbye. I'd not given her the chance to say goodbye. Dearest Mum had gone. Gone from me. And in that moment, at the cell door, I started to feel . . .

ULTRAVIOLENCE
(IT GETS YOU)

Time wasn't a problem. I'd become an expert at loading a pipe, smoking it quickly and hiding it again. I could do it in seconds rather than minutes.

I'd been back on the wing for quite some time. I knew I couldn't stay on the Fraggle Wing forever. I would have sunk deeper into myself and my mind would not have stood a chance of repair. Although I was ill, I could still occasionally reason with myself and behave in a way that could be seen as progress.

Miss Rogers was a great help to me. But seeing Dad and Adam, learning my mum's fate, had made me see things different. It had reminded me that there was life on the outside. That things carried on. I'd stopped myself from thinking about that because I knew it would make it more difficult for me inside. It would be too painful. Seeing them wasn't the moment that would be my epiphany, but it was something that gave me strength to have a new focus – escape.

I still couldn't get through the day without smack and crack, though.

Being told that Mum had died crushed me. It felt as if every ounce of me had evaporated. To know I would never see her again was more than I could bear. I became more of a recluse, if that was possible. I refused exercise and even refused to wash. I just sat inside my four walls, driving myself deeper into despair. The funeral was arranged and I was entitled to go – but only if I had God knows how many armed police and prison officers escorting me. I WAS NOT going to turn my mum's funeral into a circus. NO WAY. I chose not to go.

I started dreaming about going to Mum's grave. To say goodbye in person. I fantasised about being able to walk outside the prison gates. Taste freedom. Why should I wait for parole? Do the whole sentence? I decided that I wouldn't. Sitting in my cell in the Fraggle Wing I promised myself that I would escape. I had no idea how I was going to do it. No one had escaped from the prison in decades. NO ONE. It was an impossible task.

I took heed of what Dad said, though. I decided to go with

the flow. Do as I was told. I knew that was the only way to get back on to a normal wing. It was the only way I would have a chance to attempt escape.

With my newfound obedience – biting my tongue and swallowing my meds – and with the help of Miss Rogers, it wasn't long before I was downgraded from eight screws to six. Six to four and so on. Eventually I was allowed to exercise with the others, then associate with them as well. And finally, once I'd proved myself able to do those things while on the Fraggle Wing, they decided to relocate me to A Wing.

I was introduced to my new cellmate Terry, who was a pretty good lad. Quiet and handy if he needed to be. He was a user who seemed fine as long as he was out of his head. His night terrors would sometimes get on my tits. A pipe or a clump usually sorted it out, though.

Even though I had a new 'plan', I still struggled to be patient. I couldn't be around just anyone. I was still violent. I slipped back into my old job of watching Tommo's back. I needed drugs and that was the easiest way to get them. I also needed to vent some anger, and that was the best way of releasing it. I was a little more discreet this time, that's all. Only a little, mind.

My plan to escape was the only thing that kept me focused. Once I got back on the wing, I decided to play the game as best I could with the screws. Try to blend in a bit better. Not go against the grain with them as much. My dad was right about that. It served me well. But not in the way he'd have hoped.

I managed to get myself a job in the workshops. Most of the screws didn't give a shit what my motives were, they just seemed happy my violence towards them and the system had improved.

Terry had also got a job in the shops, not that he went all that often. After exercise, we'd have a few pipes and that would normally be enough to knock him out and send him to sleep. Sleep was his bird killer. He'd roamed around the prison system for years. Jail to jail. He wasn't a problem to the staff. He was a junkie, a stone-head. He didn't give a fuck where they ghosted him. He didn't really have much family and didn't care about seeing the ones he did have. When they wanted to move him, he didn't complain. Nearly everyone else does because they don't want to be moved too far from their families. Makes sense. Terry, he was different. He was a traveller of jails. He was one of those cons who get shipped from pillar to post because he doesn't put up a fight. He went where they said, end of. The service would move him in order to fill beds. More importantly, balance graphs and audits.

Terry and I rushed back to our cell for a quick pipe before workshops. I'd taken my lot of brown and white already, and was feeling the high.

'Hurry up, they'll be letting us out in a minute,' I said to Terry. He fucked around with it, taking ages to get it done.

'Give it here!' I said, in a playful way.

We heard the doors starting to open. They were unlocking for shops and sowsh. I loaded the pipe to the top, packing it tight and neat. The noise of the doors opening was getting louder. Closer. Terry grabbed the pipe, I lit the gear. He toked on it hard, puffing like his eyes were going to pop out of his head.

'Hurry up!' I screamed.

Puff puff, cough cough. They were only a door away. Last puff, pipe behind the bog and the door swung open. Cramfield stood there in all his fat glory. Terry was coughing like a maniac. Like he was fucking dying.

There was a smell of burning in the cell and a slight mist. When you smoke crack, the smoke is totally different to that of fags and weed. It disburses much more quickly but because we'd cut it so close to the wire, there was still a smell of burning.

'The fuck's wrong with him?' Cramfield said.

'He's all right, Guv, just smoked a bit too quick.'

'I know that, Sommers, smoking what was my question.' And a rhetorical one, at that.

Terry got to grips with himself, stumbled over to the sink and had a quick cup of water. Cramfield just stared.

'Come on, you daft sod, let's go!' I tried to hurry Terry along.

We both started to walk out of the cell. Terry got out, Cramfield stopped me.

'I know what you're up to, Sommers, so don't think you're pulling the wool over my eyes.'

As he said it, I started to laugh. He stood there looking serious, trying to bog me out. The more he did, the more I laughed. The drugs had kicked in.

'Don't laugh at me, you cunt. Everyone is leaving you alone. They think you're just getting your nut down. Not me. You're a fucking slag, Sommers. You ain't changing. You're on the fucking gear and serving people who fuck with your muggy little gang.'

'Sorry, Guv,' I said, through broken laughs, 'you got the wrong inmate. Just doing my bird.' I revelled in my cheek.

He stepped closer, invading my personal space.

'Think you're above it, yeah? Reckon that Bible basher of a dad would be proud, huh?' My laughter stopped. 'Or what about that rich brother of yours? Think he'd be impressed?'

'Goad me all you want, but you got fuck all on me and never will have. I can do what the fuck I want, right under your nose.' I felt my fist beginning to clench.

'You do nothing, Sommers; you're a dirty fucking worm to me. You're a disgrace; gutless in every sense of the word.' He was very calm and collected.

'How do ya work that one out?' Fuming. The crack had taken over. I was ready to fight.

'I mean, look at it this way,' he said, 'you didn't even have the guts to go to your fucking dead mum's funeral.'

That was it. No more. NO MORE. I lunged at Cramfield. He floored me fast, with two boxer blows to my bread basket. Down to my knees, I went. BANG! He punched me on my temple, knocking me to the ground. His boots then got to work on my already winded guts.

After all the years and the notoriety I'd built, the fights I'd had, Cramfield was still not intimidated by me, not one bit.

'I know what you are, you dirty, junkie cunt. Giving it the fucking big'un. You think you're it. Newsflash, you're not. Just remember who's got the fucking keys.'

He walked off leaving me in a pile. He wanted to show he was in charge. That he was the boss. No matter what kudos I carried, it held no weight with him. He showed me, all right. Cramfield was one hard bastard. We loathed each other but the man could fight and he had the bottle of a warrior. He gave me a good shoeing that day.

I picked myself off the ground and brushed my clothes down. My ribs ached. My temple had started to swell. He knew how to punch.

'LAST CALL WORKSHOP!' I heard the screw on the Ones scream.

Shit. I had to run down. Last thing I wanted was to be left on the wing. I'd end up rolling around the floor with Cramfield and one thing I couldn't do was let things go. As he couldn't with me. As much as he wasn't scared of me, I wasn't scared of him either. We recognised each other's violent capabilities. There was no love lost, but there was a connection. We'd spent many years in each other's company. Even if you don't want to, you're forced to become familiar with each other.

I jogged out of the cell, wincing as I did so. I rubbed my ribs and guts as I jogged. Each slam of my feet sent a vibrating split up to my head, making the pain worse. I saw Cramfield going about his business. He saw me and stared. Normally he'd piss himself laughing if he saw me in any discomfort, especially if he was the one who'd caused it. That time there was no laughter, no evil stares. Nothing.

I jogged down as best I could. The wing was noisy as everyone started to come out for sowsh. The echoes, the shouts. The smell, the dirt. It's a football match. A riot. A squat. A death.

The queue for the shop had all but gone. The shop screw waiting at the door was Mr Wise. I was pleased to see him on the workshop. He was laid back. Chilled.

'Hurry up, Davey boy!' he yelled.

'Sorry, Guv, had to have a chat with Mr Cramfield.'

'Looks like it,' he said, pointing to my swollen temple.

I looked up and saw Cramfield leaning over the railings, staring down at us. He was giving Mr Wise a filthy look for pointing at my injury. Mr Wise noticed it as well, so he quickly rubbed me down and sent me outside. There were more cons than usual waiting to go over.

'Why so many, Guv?' I asked Mr Wise.

'The packing contract has got to be finished – we need some extra lads.'

Made sense. The job only involved putting plastic cases together and chucking them into a box – it wasn't rocket science. I don't know what they were, or who they were for but I did it, like everyone else. Menial tasks for the big companies. We had probably fallen behind because none of us worked particularly hard. There were showers over there and, as it was so close to the yard, sometimes they'd let us out for a break. It was also pretty big, so there was plenty of room to deal gear and smoke, if you were quick enough. I was quick enough.

I looked round and saw Tommo.

'What you doing out here?' He didn't come that often. When he did, I normally knew about it before.

'Gonna be loads over there today, blood. Be a good time to knock out some stuff.'

'Why didn't you tell me? How can I watch ya back, if I don't know what you're up to?'

'I did come to tell ya, but I saw Cramfield giving you a "talking" to.'

'A cunt, that fella,' I said, rubbing my gut, 'but, fuck me, his chats have a nasty way of causing bruises!'

We both laughed. My and Cramfield's rivalry was common knowledge among the cons and staff alike. Sometimes I'd win, sometimes I'd lose. I'd lost that day.

Terry was standing next to me, not looking the brightest

I'd ever seen him. He had a dozy-looking grin slapped on his boat; that and some dribble seeping from his mouth and his watery, bloodshot eyes.

'You all right, son?' I asked, putting my arm around him.

He half grinned and nodded yes. That power smoke had fucked him up. Crack has an intense, strong and euphoric high. It can give you the strength of ten men, or at least make you think that you have. Crack, though, like any drug, gives you the appearance and communication skills of a cabbage if you do too much, or too quickly. The copious amounts of weed and smack that we'd done that morning hadn't helped either.

I felt the pains in my body from the Cramfield event. God only knows how I'd have felt if I'd been straight. I walked around in a drug-induced haze. I felt totally exhilarated every time I was about to take some drugs. Whatever it was. I would get a butterfly feeling in my stomach; a tingle in my arms. My emotions would be at a rapturous high, even before I'd inhaled my first puff. The ritual, just the knowledge of what was going to enter my system, was enough to give me a natural euphoria. The excitement of taking it was almost as intense as the high I continually searched for. Luckily I had a constant supply in Tommo. I had to. I always needed to know that I could take some if I wanted to. Tommo ensured my supply didn't run out. If it did, I would get violent and threaten even him. I'd been close to beating him. Very close indeed.

'Come on, you lazy sods, we got boxes to pack!' Mr Wise shouted over to us.

'You heard the Officer, move your arses.' Miss Dalton was the other screw working on the shop that day. The woman was fucking horrible. A real bitch. She had a vicious, moody look to her face. She barked more than spoke. She had an attitude with everyone. Other screws and us. No one liked her. She was fierce and I'd seen her knock out several cons. I'd also heard the stories from the staff about her drunken antics around the screws' club, beating up and fighting with her male colleagues. She'd use excessive force, in front of anyone. And she got away with it, too, because she was a woman.

Having her work shop with Mr Wise was like having Jekyll and Hyde. The one good thing about her, though, was that if you left her alone, she let you get on with it. But if you made her get up off her fat, lazy arse, that's when the bulldog would snarl.

'Fucking move it, then!' she screamed.

There was a load of mumbling – 'fat bitch', 'dyke cunt', 'slag should have some cock'. The group of us started to walk slowly. I was at the back. We did the normal walk round the yard, heading towards the shop. The usual shouts were heard from B Wing windows. I literally had to carry Terry. Smashed is an understatement.

As we walked around the yard, I looked up at the CCTV pole. I looked at it standing there to attention, in all its glory.

I smiled to myself. I was filled with excitement at the prospect of my future. A future I had mapped out in my mind. A future on the other side of the wall. All I had to do was get up that pole and I was out. I didn't know how I was going to do it yet, but I knew I was going to climb the bastard thing and get out. I knew how bad security was. How lax. Although it was a tough plan to carry out, I never for one second thought that I wouldn't make it. I needed to believe I was getting out of this shit hole.

I didn't think beyond that. I didn't think of how I'd live, or where. I didn't even think about how I was going to pay my National Insurance or what the drawbacks would be if I needed medical attention. No practical thoughts came into my head. All I thought about was being on the other side of the wall. Living my life as I chose. Beating the system. And I had a burning desire to visit Mum's grave. I was still haunted by memories. I still thought about her all the time. People knew that, too, hence the Cramfield goading. They'd heard about my visit with Dad and Adam. They'd heard about my breaking down on the Fraggle Wing. No one dared say anything to me. No one except Cramfield.

We got to the door of the shop and went in, one by one. The place looked like a cross between an airbase hanger and a factory. It had several large tables, which we all sat around, doing our work. It had exposed brickwork walls and electric heaters hanging from the ceiling. Right at the far end was a corridor that led to the showers and toilets. That's where we'd hang out, deal, fight and go for a shit. The screws sat near the front door, drinking tea, eating cakes, getting fat. I'm sure they were supposed to check what was going on, but they rarely did. Don't blame them. I wouldn't fancy checking a shower full of convicts taking drugs. As long as there were plenty of blokes left doing a bit of work, we were mostly left alone.

There were shit loads of materials that needed to be packed. More than there'd been before. I could see why they needed more blokes. Not that they were all there to pull their fingers out. More like pull their pipes out.

We took our seats and started 'work'. Tommo was quick to head to the corridor; he had plenty of gear to push. I wasn't long after him. Muscle and all that. Terry got on with some work, as did most of the lads. One by one, they gradually filtered through for the toilet, or to see Tommo. It didn't take long for him to get rid of all the gear he had.

I headed back to the tables. I was getting pissed off. Most of us were. We were actually being made to work. Hard. There was still a shit load more to do and Dalton was screaming her ugly head off every two seconds.

'Hurry up, you lazy bastards, we got to get this lot out. Stop fucking around!'

'All right, luv, this ain't *Full Metal Jacket*!' Terry said, under his breath. Not usually known for his spontaneity or quick sense of humour, that really made us laugh. Good job the bulldog didn't hear. She came up behind me.

'You had a shower yet, Sommers?'

'No, Miss, why?'

'We got some lads coming in from another wing to help get this shit finished. I'd go and have one now if I was you, or you might not get a chance.'

Very civil. Perhaps she was a lady after all.

'Tommo, can I borrow your shower gel and towel?'

'Yeah, bruv,' he looked at me, confused.

'Dyke Dalton's letting me have a shower!'

'Ahhh, she wants a bit of dangerous Davey, huh?'

'Behave, ya cunt!'

I grabbed the stuff and walked to the showers. I looked round laughing at them all still working, giving the wanker sign.

I'd been in the shower for ages. I was the only one in there. I'd had a long soak. Not that they were power showers or anything, but they were the best in the nick. They had tough, plastic floors, dirty, grey walls and it stank of piss and shit and was filthy. The showers, though, ran at a comfortably warm temperature. Most of the showers at The Well were either scalding or freezing. In there, they were just right.

I'd just finished drying myself down. I'd put my boxers and jogging bottoms on. I sat for a minute at one of the benches, just taking my time. I was still bare-chested and putting my socks on when the shower door opened and four geezers walked in. I looked up but didn't take much notice of them. Just carried on about my business.

'You not going to say hello, then?' said a gravelly voice.

I stared at his feet. Big fucking feet they were, too. I carried on up his body to his face. Standing over me was a black geezer with only one eye. Casey.

I'd not seen him in years. Not since Donnie and I had taken over.

Casey was never a man to go down easily. Never. The showdown happened with a huge fight between me and Casey. In the struggle he pulled a knife. I pulled a gun and blew one of his kneecaps to smithereens. He tried to stab me and I turned his knife on him, slicing his face all the way from his false eye to his mouth.

He was beaten. I gave him the talk. Told him I'd better not see him again, or he'd find a bullet in his nut next time. Donnie and I left him in a pool of his own blood, hailing ourselves as the new bosses.

I'd not seen him since that day. I'd had no idea if he'd bled to death, moved on, got nicked or what. Sitting in that shower room in the workshop, I got my answer. He'd obviously built up another crew somewhere else. He was inside, for one thing, and the geezers he had with him weren't boy scouts, for another.

He still wore the battle wounds from our last meet. His face had a thick scar all the way down it. It was more than a scar. It was a fucking valley. A deep crevice of grey, dead skin that looked like it hadn't healed but just died. He slouched over, leaning on one leg, obviously carrying a long-term disability from having his kneecap blown off. I didn't know if it was a plastic kneecap, a prosthetic leg or if nature had been kind. I sure wasn't about to ask. As he stepped a bit nearer, I saw the difficulty he had walking.

I should have been worried. Scared. But I wasn't. I felt numb. High. Fucked. I wasn't even particularly shocked to see him. But I did know I was going to have to work extremely hard to get out of there alive.

'Go on, then, say something. All these years and you don't so much as say hello?' He stepped nearer again, this time standing really close.

'What do you want from me?' I said. 'How you been doing? The family keeping well? What's the fucking point, Casey, huh?'

I knew his methods. He always started with small talk. Friendly. Then he'd turn. I wasn't going to follow his lead. I was more the silent type. The fear of what was coming did the trick for me. It made small talk unnecessary.

'I've known this guy, what, over twenty years, and he can't even have a chat with me?' he said to his cronies.

'Twenty years, yeah, not that I've seen you in more than fifteen. And we both know why, don't we? So let's just fucking get on with this, right?' I stood up forcefully. Mental. Even when I was on the back foot, I became the aggressor.

'WHOA! Look at you, the big Davey Sommers. The tough man that fears no one. I knew what you were capable of. You showed me, didn't you.' He pointed to his face and leg. 'I've heard your name mentioned over the years. This big-time, smart-looking fucker with plenty of dollars and everyone in his pocket. Then I come in here, hear your name mentioned again. Yeah, you're feared all right. Feared by everyone. But the rumours are different, Davey. Different, you see. People who once envied you, do you know what they say now?'

'Enlighten me?'

'Davey's dirty junkie scum. He had everything and threw it away to become a lowlife. Shit on the shoes of everyone. People don't envy you anymore. No, they loathe you. You are nothing in here, Davey. No cunt likes you. Everyone wants a sick dog to be put down. And here I am, Davey, coming to do everyone a favour . . .'

The four blokes who were with Casey started to close in tight around him, getting closer to me. Casey took a step back. I lifted my fist and got in the ready position. I knew what I had to do. I knew what they were going to try to do. One thing was for sure, I wasn't going down without a fight.

'I thought all my Christmases had come at once when I heard you were here. I knew I'd repay you for what you did to me. No cunt gets away with doing that to me. NO ONE, you hear?' His voice was rising as he stepped out of the way of his men. 'Then when I was offered the opportunity to come over here by the screws, I jumped at the chance! They knew our history and knew what I wanted to do to you.'

The four blokes got closer. I weighed them up. They all stared for a second, working me out. Trying to intimidate me. My leg shook, my fists wobbled – adrenaline poured through my veins. The voices screamed. I was ready. READY.

I didn't have to make the first move. One of the blokes stepped in and swung at me. BANG! I smashed him in the jaw before he got too close. Two more came. I punched with everything I had. I managed to hold them off for a few seconds. Before long, though, I had all four of them on me. Punching. Kicking. Blood soon began to pour out of my face, all over me. It was like one of the showers was running red. I tried to stay on my feet. That was my objective. That was the only thought I had. If I hit the deck, it was game over.

They had me up against the wall, smashing me. I felt a sharp pain rush through my calf. Before I could acknowledge it, I was on my knees. My head was cracked against the bench I'd been sitting on. Over and over. The blood now was a thick, treacle red. It was like syrup.

I was barely conscious as I slumped to the floor. They stopped for a second. Casey came into eyeshot. He was grinning from ear to ear, loving what was being done to me. He stood the glorious victor over the cunt Davey Sommers.

He pulled something out of his pocket, as did the rest of the men. I knew straight away what it was. A toothbrush – except where the brush should have been there were two blades that had been melted into the plastic. The blades were parallel to each other so that when someone was cut, there would be double slices, making it impossible for the wound to be stitched. A nasty weapon that's often used inside.

They each had one and they stood over me, laughing. I tried with all my energy to get to my feet, but it was impossible. Every time I made any progress, I was met with a firm kick and stamp. I was powerless. Unable to fight the retribution I was about to be served. The blood from my face had already soaked my bare chest, but that was nothing compared to what I was about to receive.

The next minute or so were utterly savage. They all dived into me, like vultures on a dead carcass. They sliced me up like a hog ready for a spit. Pain is a funny thing. I can't say that I actually felt much of what they were doing. I had an animal instinct that raced through me, telling me that it would be over soon. That I would be dead, and I'd feel no more. I shut my eyes as they tore at my body. Slice after slice. I put myself in another place.

I was at the dinner table waiting for Mum to serve up one of her legendary Sunday roasts. I was there with all the family. Adam and Dad sat next to me, making jokes, talking, idle chit chat. It's amazing what a traumatised brain can do.

The cutting stopped. My eyes opened. I'd crash-landed back to reality. I was soaked in my own blood. A pool of it lay around my body. I looked down and saw my flesh all hacked up. There was hardly any skin that hadn't been cut. I didn't panic that I might die, but rather that I might live. I was ready to go. Ready to meet my maker. I just wanted out. My chest felt tight, I was struggling to breathe. Casey leant down to me, so he was inches away from my face.

'I never did tell you how I lost my eye.' He started to laugh, before turning deadly serious. 'It was in prison.'

He thrust his blade towards my eye. My survival instinct was to reach out, catching his hand just as he did so. Yeah, I wanted to die, that's for sure. But I didn't want my eye cut out of my head.

He got on top of me, forcing the blade towards my eye. I tried with all my might to hold him off. The harder he leant in, the closer he got.

'GO ON, CASEY, DO HIM!' one of the men screamed.

He got his whole body weight on top of me. I couldn't hold him off. The blade reached my eye. It was there, on my eyeball. But still I fought, trying to stop him. He was too strong. He started to cut.

'AAAAARRRRRGGGGGHHHHH!' I screamed. The pain was intense.

'CASEY, QUICK, LET'S GO!' They pulled him off me.

Had they heard something? Had they reached the limit of the time they'd been given to do me? I don't know. But they fled. Casey hobbled out of that shower room and it was the last time I ever saw him.

I started to drift out of consciousness. My eye socket was bleeding; I could feel it running down my cheek. I didn't know what damage he'd done but my lid had firmly closed and I couldn't open it. I felt the other lid getting heavy until I was no longer conscious. Relief.

I don't know the logistics of how my assault took place. One thing's for sure, it had to have been organised. I was a marked man by several screws and cons. It was no skin off anyone's nose to see me destroyed. Maybe Tommo's because I was his muscle. But muscle in prison comes ten-a-penny.

I felt a slap around my face, which brought me back to consciousness. Mr Wise was standing over me, looking shocked and sick by what was in front of him.

'Shit, Davey... What the fuck? Don't worry, I'll get help.'

He radioed through, calling all the medics available. I was rushed straight to hospital. My injuries had resulted in me losing a hell of a lot of blood. I was put on an IV and force-fed antibiotics to take down the infection.

I was in an awful lot of pain for weeks. They couldn't stitch me. I was on high doses of painkillers and antibiotics, and twenty-four hours a day, for weeks, I was cuffed to a screw at my hospital bed, with two others sitting beside him. I was a three-man bed-watch. Not fun.

My eye had to be stitched. They said that my eyesight

'should' remain. The one thing I know is I got what I deserved. You hurt, you'll be hurt. Karma. Sometimes it's instant; sometimes it takes years, or may not even happen in this life. But one thing's for sure, it will be served.

The cell door opened and I walked in. Terry was doing his usual, lying on his bed half asleep, stoned out of his nut.

'What's happening, bruv?'

'Terry boy!' I said, shaking his hand.

'Fucking hell, mate, you got fucked. Been talk of the nick since you been in hospital. They ghosted Dalton; she's gone to work at another nick.'

'Good, the fucking fat dyke bitch.'

Don't think she ever got investigated. I never pursued it. I didn't tell the Governors who did me. I didn't see the point.

I looked out the window, at the workshop and, more importantly, at the CCTV camera and grinned.

'Back to the shop tomorrow,' I said.

'You not heard?'

'Heard what?'

'They banned anyone they think is trouble. You're top of that list.'

I looked back out of the window.

A hiccup, that was all it was; I'd still get to where I wanted to be.

'You got any gear?'

I sat back, took drugs and waited to heal properly. I

waited and watched. I did a whole lot of watching. Waiting for the time to be right and my plan to be ready. I did the training, got the strength. My bird killer, my whole focus, was to be ready to put my plan into action. Doing the big jump was going to liberate me in a way that I never thought possible . . .

THE SHINING

Mikey put his foot flat to the floor, not easing up for a second. He had to get us away, take us as far away as we could get. I didn't know how long it would be before staff at The Well realised they were a man down on the numbers. I was probably safe for a while but there was no point taking any chances. I slumped back into my seat and stared ominously out the window. How had my life reached this?

I had been chasing the elusive dream of freedom for a long time. It had been my driving force. It was what I thought I wanted. What I thought I needed. It would bring me peace. Peace with who I'd become. But the dream is always better than the reality. The longing I had to be on the outside, the yearning I felt to be on the road, didn't translate to the feeling of excited glee I was hoping for.

I looked at the world out of the window as Mikey sped through the roads. Nine years had passed since I'd been locked up. A lot changes in nine years. The world seemed alien. The car shapes had changed. The clothes of those around me. Mikey looked weird. But none of this excited me, worried me or anything. I just felt empty. What now? Where do I go? What do I do? I still carried the burden of incarceration. I still had that twisted knot of hate bubbling in my gut and I didn't know why. Freedom didn't feel like the cure to my madness that I thought it would be. Far from it.

I heard a ringing noise and Mikey pulled an object out of his back pocket and put it to his ear. It was tiny. The new revolution in mobile phones. When I was banged up only the rich and famous carried mobile phones. I'd had one, of course. Image. Rank. Position. It seemed now every fucker had them.

'Yeah, got him. Yeah, yeah. About an hour. Yeah, he needs a feed! Laters.' He hung up the phone. 'You shit your fucking self, didn't ya!?'

I was mildly embarrassed. 'Poxy little fucking things, aren't they?'

I sat back deep into my seat and drifted off. I couldn't stop thinking about Mum. How I'd not had a chance to say goodbye. I wanted to see her resting place. Spend some time with her. Talk about things, my mistakes. Tell her I loved her. Apologise for not attending her funeral.

'You wanna cheer up, don't ya? You hop the fucking wall like no other and you're sitting there miserable as sin! What's up with ya?'

'Take me to Mum's grave.'

There was a silence. Even though he hadn't been inside with me at the time, he knew how hard I'd taken it when Mum died. He used to visit me every now and then.

'Davey, mate, we can't go there just yet. It'll soon be . . .'

'I don't give a fuck what it will soon be. You take me there now!' I stared at him.

He slammed on the brakes hard, skidding to a sharp stop at the side of the road. He turned round and looked at me deep in my eyes.

'You listen here, Davey, I've risked fucking everything to come here and get you. EVERYTHING. I get caught, I'm back in the slammer. My missus finds out, she'll cut my bollocks off. I know how you feel, but I will say this once: from here on in, until I get you to safety, I MAKE THE FUCKING DECISIONS. Understand? If not, you can get the fuck out.'

He was deadly serious. He wasn't going to take my bullying shit. The look in his eye made me realise that. He was ready to whack me and shove me out on the street. One hand held the steering wheel so tight the blood had drained from his knuckles, the other was clenching. I respected him for standing his ground with me. It also dawned on me that I had no one else to trust.

'All right, Mikey, son, you win.'

He put his foot down and away we went.

'It's not like I don't want you to see ya mum, it's just gonna be fucking live with the filth any minute now. It's not safe for either of us.'

I nodded. I knew he was right. But I didn't care if I was caught. I just wanted to see Mum and then I could die, for all I cared. I didn't feel like I had a life left worth living. I was finished.

My morning take of drugs was starting to wear off. My body was starting to feel heavy in the seat. I was aware of every ache and pain in my body. The climb was only part of the strain I'd put on myself. The adrenaline and fast heart rate had taken an immense toll on my body, too. The hiding, the contemplating, the pursuit of action. Everything made me feel weak. Lethargic and beaten. Along with that, my craving for a hit was returning. I was going through it bad.

When you want a hit, you pace the room. You're pulling your fucking hair out. That day, though, I had the craving, the immense sensation of wanting it, but even stronger was the severe tiredness I felt from escaping. The craving was an accompaniment to this tiredness. It was there, like the starvation it was but I was in new territory now. I didn't know what or how to feel.

I looked down at the wrist I'd landed on. It had blown up like a balloon. The minute I saw it, pain began to follow. I was in a strange state. Awake but dreamy. Real but detached. I closed my eyes and the blanket of sleep started to take hold.

I felt a vibration going through my body. Over and over it went. Bouncing. Head bopping. One eye then the other, I started to peel them open.

'Davey, wake up, bruv, we're here.' Mikey was standing over me, shaking me.

I yawned and stretched, then slowly got out of the car. As my feet touched the ground outside, I felt the crackly slip of gravel and stone. I slowly pulled myself out, feeling ever more stiff. As I stood up, Mikey had two fags in his mouth, lighting them both. He passed one to me and I began to smoke. I looked round and saw we were standing on a huge, shingle-covered driveway. Trees sat deep into the surrounding land. There was an overgrown and unkempt garden. A revolting shit-stink filled my nostrils. I looked around for the culprit.

'What the fuck is that smell?' I asked Mikey.

He was smoking his fag and pointed. I saw a pond. No, a small lake. It was greeny brown. I'd seen a lot of ponds but none that colour before. It was different. He could see the confusion on my face.

'It's stagnant, that's what makes the fucking stink round here.'

Even the water was dead in my presence. I scanned the area. It was big. Fucking big. That's when I saw the building. It looked like a decaying old manor, a country house of some sort. It looked fucked, like the rest of the place. Most of the windows were boarded up and it was obvious that it had been done a long time ago. The wood looked old. The windows that weren't covered were makeshift plastic types and badly fitted. There were no neighbours, or even any bloody roads, by the looks of things. It was deep in the woods, in the middle of nowhere.

'I've hooked you up here, bruv. It's a top squat. It's like it's off the fucking radar. They've been here for fucking years, man. Got it nailed down good. They got generators and all sorts. It's mega!'

Mikey's attempt at being upbeat didn't raise my spirits. I was emotionless.

We walked up to the front door, climbing the half dozen concrete steps that led to it. It was massive, made of oak and covered in graffiti, carvings and mistreatment. There were burn stains at the bottom. Mikey knocked on the door several times. It took a while to open. Once it did, though, it was like Dracula's den being revealed.

'Hi, Mikey, you must be Davey?' She put out her hand.

'All right,' I said, shaking it.

'I'm Josie, pleased to meet ya.'

'Likewise,' I couldn't muster many words.

She had a greasy mullet that was dyed several different

colours. Her face was covered in piercings. Her nose, ears, lips, cheeks – everything had metal hanging from it. She wore silky, tie-dyed wraparound clothing that didn't hide her malnourished and emaciated physique.

We walked inside and were hit in the face by a damp smell of piss. The tiles on the floor were cracked and dirty, the walls were covered in weird paintings. Some were graffiti, others seemed to be the grotesque drawings of someone as high as a kite. There was a fucking great big staircase in the middle of the entrance hall, with three large reception rooms off it. Apart from the smell and, of course, the décor, it was remarkably clean. Josie led the way. I peered into the rooms off the hall as we went – one was smoke filled, with the sound of a couple of men talking. The next was dark with psychedelic lights flashing non-stop and the subtle bump of sombre trance music. The third room was shut.

We walked through an archway, which led us into the kitchen. The smell of sausages, eggs and bacon frying filled my nostrils. I breathed in deep. I felt a warm sensation of childhood bliss. I was immediately taken back to Mum and Dad's kitchen, watching Mum prepare the food. I craved the life and surroundings of my childhood, more than anything else. Not the glamour or money of my gangster life. Just to return to innocence and live the loving life of normality.

The kitchen was huge. Not that it was a working kitchen

in the typical sense. There was no running water and the old cooker that was left there looked like it hadn't worked in centuries. Instead there was the highest spec camping appliances, on top of the original appliances. There were gallons of Evian water everywhere and the humming sound of a generator out the back. I was impressed with how they'd arranged the place.

'Good set up, you got here. I like it.'

'Thanks, Davey.' She smiled.

'Been here ten years, she has,' Mikey informed me.

'Twelve actually.'

'How come you don't get fucked off out of here?'

'We came here to squat years ago and, as it's in the middle of nowhere, it was kind of overlooked. We've been here more than ten years now, so I think we might actually own it by law!' She laughed, but was serious.

'Why don't you find out and sell it, or do it up?' I asked.

'What's the point? We could be wrong and I don't want to force the issue and get the authorities to kick us out. I shut up and they say nothing, so here we are.'

She had a point. Living the life of a hippy without worries.

'Don't ya get loads of other people trying to come and squat here?'

'Did at first, not anymore. Gerry, my fella, has been working for Mikey for some time now. Since then, we threw out everyone we didn't want; making everyone aware it was our place. People that are here now, are here cos we want them to be.'

Mikey was obviously the muscle behind it. I didn't ask in what capacity Gerry worked for Mikey. Didn't need to know. Didn't want to know. My guess was pushing drugs or collecting debts. Most likely a combination of both.

'I'm wanted then, huh?' I said, half smiling.

'Mikey talks very highly of you. Told us everything about your situation. A friend of Mikey's is a friend of ours. In all honesty, I didn't think you'd make it. When he said you're banged up in The Well and that you were going to hop it, I never really thought you'd do it. He never doubted you, though.'

We both looked at Mikey who seemed embarrassed. My wrist was throbbing, my body was aching. Josie tended the food.

'I take it you want a good feed, right?'

'Most definitely.'

I was hungry. Hungrier than I'd been in years. The smell of good food cooking wasn't something I'd had for nearly a decade. The slop at The Well wasn't like a freshly cooked fry up. The smell took me away from my situation for a short while. Transcended me back home.

There was a huge bong set on top of the table. Mikey clocked me staring at it.

'Have a go.'

He threw me a large bag of green. Perfect to help numb the pain a little and give me the munchies.

'You mind if I do?' I asked Josie.

'Knock yourself out,' she answered, while tending the eggs frying in the pan.

I smoked hard and fast, getting as much inside me as I could. Before I'd even had time to cough, she had put the largest plate of grub in front of me I'd ever seen. I got stuck in like it was the first meal I'd ever eaten. Every bite tasted magical. The sausage, egg and ketchup-smothered food slid down my neck. I was sitting round the table with my family. Laughing, joking. I was there. REALLY THERE. I was taken back twenty-five years. I was talking to them, enjoying them, being with them.

'Can I have another egg, please, Mum?'

Mikey pissed himself laughing. CRASH! And I was back in the room. I was back in the squat.

'You want another egg, luv?' Josie asked.

'No, ta, I'm fine.' I was embarrassed.

I finished the food. Josie, Mikey and I sat around getting stoned. Conversation flowed, but I didn't really engage. My craving for some harder stuff was getting stronger.

'Mikey, mate, I need some brown and white, badly.'

'Come on,' Josie said, taking my hand.

We left the kitchen and went in the room with the door that was closed. As she opened it, I saw what was inside. It looked like a clinic or doctor's surgery. It was very clean and sterile. There was even hand wash to be used as I walked in. There weren't any chairs; instead, there were square beanbags, set neatly all the way round the edge of the room. Each one had a small table next to it. There were four or five people in there, all cooking up drugs to inject. There was even a fucking needle bin.

'There's no excuse for filthy germs and sharing needles. We won't have it here. Everyone can take what they want, but it's done professionally.'

Mikey had a nice little enterprise here. A proper crack and smack house. Not your usual filth. Not the normal dirty crack den you see in the papers or on TV. It was a professional outfit.

One of the blokes shooting up was well dressed and in a suit. Another looked like a builder. There was a middle-aged woman who looked every bit the average housewife. I was the most junkie-looking out of everyone. I'd not even changed out of my prison kit.

'Take a seat over there, Davey.'

I sat down and looked around the room. Mikey came in.

'I'm chipping off. Have a good time and I'll be back later. Josie's got some clobber for you to change into, once, ya know...' He nodded his head, indicating once I was high.

Josie came over to me with a little leather case, sat down beside me and started to get out some materials from inside. There was heroin and crack, a set of needles and cooking-up tools.

'Smoking it will do,' I said.

She just smiled and continued with the cooking-up ritual. Before I knew it, the needle was full of crack and heroin.

'You ever done a speedball?' she asked.

'I smoke H and C together, if that counts.'

'Not quite. You're gonna love this. Clench your fist.'

She forced the needle into a vein in my arm and pushed every bit of the liquid into me. The hit was almost instant. It was like nothing I'd ever experienced before. My body went totally limp and my vision went double. I felt a pull at my feet and at my arms. A gentle tug stretching me. My hearing echoed and everything seemed to go in slow motion.

Josie looked at me and laughed. Her laugh sounded deep, slow and shook through my whole body. She helped me to my feet. I looked around the room; my brain was unable to process what my eyes were seeing at the same rate, so it became a freeze-frame picture. I felt higher than I'd ever felt. More wrapped up in the heroin blanket than I had ever thought possible. Injecting it gave me an entirely different hit. More intense, more exotic.

She walked me out of the room. The hallway looked bigger and then smaller. I felt huge, then tiny. I was experiencing a flurry of hallucinations that were totally hypnotic. There was a man standing in the hallway. He had a thick beard and long straggly hair. He wore a leather jacket and looked like a rocker.

'D-a-v-e-y——m-e-e-t——G-e-r-r-y...' Josie's speech was difficult for my brain to register and I heard it in long, drawn-out syllables.

We shook hands. I must have looked smashed. He laughed and it felt like a fucking earthquake rattling through my bones.

'T-a-k-e——h-i-m——i-n——t-h-e-r-e . . .' he said to Josie.

She walked me into the psychedelic room. We got closer and the lights flashed hard. They penetrated deep into my brain. I felt like I was a part of the lights. They were inside me. The bass from the stereo pumped through me. The lights flickered so much they nearly knocked me off my feet. Josie held me up – no mean feat for someone built like a field-mouse.

There was a group of people in the middle of the room, falling dancing to the music, who looked equally fucked. She put me at the side of the room, where I slumped into a chair. She turned on her heels and walked out, looking back, smiling as she did so. I sat there, comatose, feeling as though I didn't exist. Like I was floating through the air. Like I was the air. I didn't feel real. I was stuck. Paralysed.

A speedball is probably the most deadly combination of drugs and injecting it is the most deadly way of taking it. I don't know the exact odds, but you have an extremely high chance of dying instantly. It's a killer, all right. It's the ultimate high and you're risking the ultimate price.

Everyone experiences drugs in different ways – that afternoon, after taking the speedball, I was all over the place. The state my mind was in when I'd taken it contributed to my transient state.

The room seemed to rush past me; then everything stood still. The music felt good; then it felt like the devil trying to pull my soul downstairs. Sometime later, Josie came in and sat next to me. She had a glaze to her eyes, too, by then. She looked more than stoned. She'd been back to the closed door room. She had a painful grin and was pulling an awkward face. She looked uglier than anyone I'd ever seen. As I stared, I broke her face down into shapes. She looked like a witch. An angel. What was left of my mind was turning to mush.

I don't know how long I sat there. Eventually Josie's face returned to a slightly more regular state. She led me out of the trippy room, into the first smoke-filled room. Gerry was in there with a small crowd of people. There were bongs and spliffs being smoked. There was a mountain of Charlie on the coffee table and an assortment of pills next to it. They were all different colours and I didn't have a clue what they were.

'There you go, mate.' Gerry gave me a bottle of beer.

I'd not tasted one in years. It was bitter sweet. Sickly. I didn't enjoy it. I was passed a spliff which I smoked quickly. I was passed one pill after another, all different colours. I didn't give a shit what they were. Gerry quietly strummed on a guitar, smoking away.

I sat back and smoked a bong with Josie. It wasn't long before I was rushing out of my mind. The genetically modified weed and the exotic pills shot my brain into another dimension.

Once I got to a certain level of intoxication, drugs all felt similar to me. I was taking so much and I was well and truly fucked out of my mind. They took away my self-reflection. The voices.

Josie and I went back into the trippy room. I took the same seat and stared into space, unable to talk. Changing shapes, floating, dying, screams, whispers, anger, hatred, love, care, loathe, fly. FLY. FLY. FLY. I wasn't real.

Josie took me back to the closed door room. Speedball. Trippy room. Smoke and pills. Trippy room. Speedball. Trippy room. Smoke and pills. Trippy room. Over and over. I don't know how long it carried on. Five hours, five days, I just can't remember. I don't remember sleeping, I don't remember being awake. Like a blink, I found myself standing naked under a drizzle of cold water. My hair was drenched, my body wet. My beard was knotted. I was staring at a wall of broken tiles. I looked around, trying to find out where I was and how I got there. I was in a rusty, old bath, under a makeshift shower – a clear plastic bag, full of water, with a shower head attached to it. There was a valve, which you turned to release the water.

I tried to get my bearings, find out why I was there. Nothing was coming to me. The water hit my head slowly; I stared at the broken tiles in front of me.

'AARRGGHH!'

A flashback hit me, like a punch in the face. I jumped back. A flashback of me hurting someone.

My normal sight came back.

Then again.

'ARRGGHH.'

Snapshots of pain. Of violence. Me dishing out cruelty. Flashbacks from my past. I was there. A spectator. Watching, hating everything I witnessed. Each flashback I saw I felt the pain of the victim I was torturing.

My heart rate rose to a frightening level. I was scared. Out of control. Being taken over. Reduced to the minuscule germ that I was. I jumped out of the shower. I was dying. DYING. Everything I thought I wanted was happening. I'd prayed to be taken. Prayed to leave this world. My heart was jumping out of my chest; my breathing was out of control. Every hair on my body stood to attention.

And every few seconds, another flashback came.

'PLEASE, NO!' I screamed.

I felt like a coward. I wanted them to stop. I couldn't face them. I was too scared to analyse my feelings.

One after another, visions appeared, knocking me off my feet as they did so. What was happening? Death was surely around the corner. It was just my imagination. Every time I had a vision, I became blind. Blind to the physical world.

I thought I knew what I had done. I thought I knew my life. I didn't. Now I could see the ego-driven way I had behaved. Could see it for what it was. The hatred, the selfish desire to live a rich and illicit life. The hurt and pain I had caused.

I scrambled to find my clothes. My prison kit was on the floor. Wet. Stinking. On with the clothes: damp, wet, dirty. I was in agony. Fearful pain. Scared. Deranged. Anxious. Run. I must run. RUN. I couldn't pull the clothes on fast enough. I felt the full flow of adrenaline, like never before. So strong from the inside, I could barely feel a touch on my skin. It was like all my nervous energy, even the nerves themselves, had sunk deep into my body. Everything was there, trying to cope with the rushes I was having.

I ran out of the bathroom, which took me to the top of the stairs. It was dark. Everywhere was pitch black. It was night, that much I realised.

'ARRGGHH!'

Knives, guns, bats. Punches, cuts, maim. The vision smacked me so hard in the face I fell halfway down the stairs. I jumped to my feet. RUN. RUN. I ran down to the bottom of the stairs. I could hear a few people talking, obviously still partying. I didn't stop. I had to go. I had to get out of there. I didn't know where I was going, just away. Away from the building. Away from myself. I was heading to hell. I was feeling the wrong side of my own iron fist.

I smashed through the front door, clearing the half dozen

steps the other side. I stumbled on to my hands, grazing them as I did so. Even though I had a fractured wrist, I felt nothing. I couldn't even remember the escape, let alone the injury I picked up doing it.

I ran deep into the night, jerking the whole time, flooded with a plethora of images and pain. I ran aimlessly into the woods. Unable to find my direction. Unable to gauge what I was running away from. It was torture. The most scared I'd ever felt. Fight had been my way. Never flight. But I was running now. I couldn't stop. I was breathing heavier than I'd ever breathed before. I was screaming like I was being chased by a starved lion. I was running from myself. Running from the life I'd led. I wanted to burst out of my skin. Get away. Forget.

Exhaustion got the better of me and I collapsed in a heap, whimpering. Jerking sporadically like a newborn, I fell asleep. I don't know what followed. A dream or conscious-ness – somewhere in between. Once again, I had a flashback. A flashback of one of the many conversations I'd had with Mum; one that she would have with me, from time to time, about my lifestyle. The way I was. She was worried and concerned and would offer me several ideas of how I could change myself. Though, she never once said better myself. She always saw me as a good person. A ray of light that had potential to lead a good life. I'd humour her. I was polite, courteous. She was my mum. She would talk to me about family values, the good that is inside all human beings, that everyone had the potential to be kind. She believed that all anyone had to do was wake up to it. Look at the world around, see the true nature of life.

I let her say what it was she needed to say. I never listened. She always said, though, that one day I would. One day I'd hear. Lying in that wood, I heard every word. Every word of Mum's advice. I listened. I heard. And I screamed, over and over, calling her name.

Alone with my mind, lying there in the woods, I learned more about who I was than I ever had before in my life.

Day started to break. My prison garb was damp with dew; my beard itched with an insect crawling in it. I looked up at the trees, the sky. It was a mild morning. I breathed the fresh air. I looked around.

I felt different. The visions had stopped. I wasn't saved – I was still a drug addict, after all. But for the first time since I could remember, I felt delight at being alive. The hallucinations, the visions and dark reminiscences were, I'm sure, partly a by-product of my extended binge. But, what I had experienced, whatever induced it, was very, very real. It was an epiphany, a revelation, enlightenment or however you choose to label it. I call it the beginning of change. The start of me. Of being David. It was the first time I could see life for what it was. And that everything I'd done up to that point was my ego, my enemy, temptation talking to me, feeding off my bad actions. I wasn't cured but it was a start.

I got up off the floor and brushed myself down. I felt sad and elated at the same time. I felt like I'd stepped out of the darkness. I felt regret. I think it was the first time in my life I'd ever really felt that. I regretted hurting all the people I had hurt. Regretted everything I'd broken. I couldn't believe I'd gone through life causing such destruction. I felt like I'd wasted so much of my life. This wonderful gift of life.

I had to get to Dad. I had to see Mum. I needed to speak to them both. That's all I knew for sure.

It was very early in the morning and day had only just started to break.

I couldn't tell Mikey where I was going because I didn't know where he was. I didn't know where I was. I didn't know how to get back to the house. I was deep in the woods and all I wanted – needed – to do was get to Dad.

I started walking, trying to keep in one direction. My walk turned into a jog. A jog into a run. RUN. I sprinted as fast as my legs would carry me. I didn't feel any tiredness. Just determination.

Within forty minutes or so, I got to a small village. It was busy, which was good. I tried to go unnoticed, which was difficult wearing prison garb that was soaking wet and filthy. I spotted a phone box tucked under a huge overhanging oak tree. The door closed tight behind me. It was an old red phone box, so the windows were small, which gave me an extra sense of protection. I felt a little more invisible. I picked the receiver up and was about to dial but I couldn't remember the number. My mind went totally blank. I placed the receiver back down. A car drove past on the road next to me. I squeezed tight into the corner of the box, trying to conceal myself.

'Think,' I said to myself.

I closed my eyes, putting my index finger and thumb on my forehead. Finally it came to me. I quickly dialled the operator, before I could forget.

'Good morning . . .'

'Sorry – I must give you this number before I forget, it's 01 . . .'

She wrote it down.

'OK, sir, how can I help you?'

'Did you get that number OK?'

'Yes.' She was growing a little impatient.

'Great. I desperately need to do a reverse charges call to the number I've just given you, please.' I was shaking.

'OK, sir. What is the name of the person at that number, and who shall I say is calling?'

'It's Mr Sommers and I'm his son, David.'

'Thank you. You will hear the call I make; should he accept the charges, you'll be connected.'

Within a few seconds, I heard a ringing tone. I had butterflies. I was shaking. Nauseous. I didn't know what to expect. How was he going to react? He had to be in. What if he wasn't? What the fuck would I do? Adam. Adam would be next. But I needed Dad. Needed his advice.

I'd had a realisation but I didn't know what I should do next. I wasn't sure how to use it. Dad was the only one who could help.

'Hello?' He was in. I could hear his voice. Relief.

'Good morning, Mr Sommers, I have your son David on the line who is requesting a reverse charges call. Do you accept the charge?'

'Erm, David? He's on the line?' He couldn't believe what he was hearing.

'Yes, sir. David is on the line.' It went silent for a few seconds. 'Do you accept the charge or not?'

'Of course, put him through.'

'Connecting you now, sir.'

Her voice went. Neither of us spoke. I didn't know what to say.

'Hello?' Dad spoke.

I couldn't answer.

'David, are you there?'

'I'm here, Dad.'

'Thank God you're OK. I've been worried sick. What, where have you been? Why did you . . . Are you OK?'

'I don't know if I'm OK, Dad. I don't know anything anymore.' I felt a lump in my throat.

'What do you mean?'

'I'm a bad man, Dad. Evil. I've done so many terrible things. The worst kind. I've hurt so many people over the years. You, Mum and Adam included.'

'That's the first time I've ever heard you say that. Where are you?'

'I don't know what to do, Dad. I saw it. Everything. I felt what I had done. How could I have . . . ?'

'David, where are you?'

'I need your help, Dad.' I wasn't listening to him.

'I will come and get you. Where are you?'

'Please help me, Dad. I'm in a village. I'm not sure where and I don't know its name.'

'I need a bit more than that.'

'I don't know, Dad. I think it took about forty minutes or an hour or so to get here from the prison. I see a large church over the other side of the road. It's massive; I can't quite see the name. It's got a clock with . . .'

'Only one hand and a pub not far from it, called The Three Horse Shoes?' he interrupted.

I looked for the pub. Bingo.

'YES! That's it.'

'I will be there as quick as I can. Go and sit in the church graveyard.'

'OK, Dad. I need some clothes.'

'Leave it to me. Now get over there and wait.'

I found a bench at the far edge of the graveyard. It was right next to a huge bush that bordered the whole place. I felt relaxed. At peace. The serenity and calm of the graveyard, the openness, gave me an inner peace and connection.

Something I'd not felt in a long time. I felt a connection. I could feel that it was a resting place for many people. It was a comforting feeling.

What I'd been through, everything that had been shown to me the previous night, made a little more sense while I sat there waiting. I even closed my eyes for a few minutes and prayed. Something I hadn't done since I was a child. It's funny how even the biggest unbelievers put their hands together in their hour of need. It's comforting. Natural. Something that happens without even thinking about it.

My eyes were shut, my mind wandered. I was comfortable. I was exonerated for now.

I felt a hand rest on my shoulder. I opened my eyes. Dad stood over me. That old, warm face was the most amazing thing I'd ever seen. My protector. The wise man. The help I needed. He was here to save me.

'Hello, son,' he said.

I jumped up and threw my arms around him tight. I was overwhelmed with happiness. 'Thank you, Dad, thank you for coming to get me.'

'You're my son, David, I'd never leave you. I've always been here.'

I hugged him once more.

'I've brought some clothes for you.'

He had a suit on a hanger, with a shirt and tie. He also had a bag with a shaving kit, soap, a pair of cordless clippers and some polished shoes.

'This is great, Dad, I need to go and wash up.'

'First put these on, so you're out of prison clothing, then we'll go into the church. You can go to the toilet and clean yourself up, while I talk to the minister.'

I got changed discreetly and Dad stuffed my prison garb in a bag. We made our way to the church entrance.

We walked in. It looked empty and quiet inside.

'Over there to your left is the toilet. Get in there. I'll wait inside the church. When you're done, wait outside. Hurry.'

I locked the door behind me. The first thing I noticed was how clean it was. It had a wiry, heavy-duty carpet, old-fashioned porcelain which was polished to a high standard, a mirror and a radiator that was burning like a furnace. I took off my jacket, shirt and tie.

First thing I did was cut my hair. I cut it down to a grade two. It had been straggly and greasy, matted into knots from years of being left alone. The clippers struggled to go through my mop at first. I had to hack at it to get the bulk off. Once I did, I gently pushed the clippers over my head until my hair was all even. I did the same with my beard. It was too long, dirty and knotted to start shaving. Bit by bit, my hair fell in the sink, practically filling it. I did my best to get most of it out and flushed it down the toilet. I picked up the rest from the floor. It wasn't perfect, but I got rid of most of it. I filled the sink with hot water, got the soap out and washed my upper body as best I could, drying myself off with the hand towel. Then I shaved my face clean with the razor Dad had brought. I got dressed again quickly, putting on my shirt, tie and jacket. I looked in the mirror, taking in my reflection. My skin was weathered, dark and rough. My complexion was chiselled and tough. My damaged eye looked off-grey and full of water. But my hair was neat, my face clean. My shirt and tie made me look like a man with some pride and decency. I looked every bit my years, plus more.

I couldn't stop thinking about Mum. I couldn't stop seeing her face smiling at me, looking on with pride at how smart I'd made myself. I could feel her happiness at me wanting to change, trying to accept what I did, face it all and live life how it was supposed to be lived.

I scanned the toilet once more, cleaning up the last few bits. I walked out, looking left and right as I did so. It was still quiet.

I got outside and Dad was there waiting.

'Did you see anyone?' I asked.

'Yes, I had a quick chat with the minister. I've met him before.'

'All OK?'

'Everything's fine, David.'

'I need to see Mum. I have to say goodbye.'

'I know,' Dad answered.

We made our way over to his car. It was the first time I felt cleansed. Like a citizen. A human being. We got in the car and Dad started to drive.

Despite everything, I was having some involuntary jerks.

'You OK, son?'

'I feel a bit ill. I've been a drug addict for some time now. Funny thing is, though, I don't feel that I need any more. I'm not craving anything but I suppose my body still wants it.'

We spoke all the way to Mum's grave. He asked me countless questions about what I'd been feeling, the thoughts I'd been having, what led to my escape and exactly what had happened the night before. I spoke frankly to him, not really taking a breath as I did so. He listened intently, giving me his wise words along the way.

He believed that everything I'd ever done, good and bad, was a part of my learning curve. It had all happened for a reason. After walking the road of treachery and hate, to come out the other side a man who could see the true nature of life was something to be proud of. I wasn't entirely there yet, but I was on the way. The path had been laid all that time before and I'd started to walk down it. It doesn't excuse the terrible things I had done, but it was all a part of my journey.

Before long we arrived at the cemetery. We walked briskly until we were at the grave.

'There, son, there's where your mum rests.'

I looked at the gravestone. The beautiful flowers around it. I was warm, glowing, but sad. I felt I'd come home. Now I could speak to her. Say the goodbye that I wanted to.

Dad left me there for some time, then came back to get me.

'David,' he said gently. 'David, we must go.'

He helped me to my feet. We walked out of the cemetery, leaving the car. Where I was going was within walking distance. I knew what I had to do.

I'd been a fugitive for eight days. Eight days since I'd escaped from prison. From the very moment I got over the wall, I didn't feel right. It didn't feel like I thought it would. Something was missing. Giving in to the craving for physical freedom, drugs or even food didn't satisfy me. In order to face my demons, to educate myself further and reach my full potential, I first had to face up to everything I'd done in the past. I had to hand myself in.

We got to the police station.

'I don't know if I can do this, Dad. I'm scared.'

'I'm with you, son. All the way. You know it's the right thing to do. You'll find solace. You'll find forgiveness. It won't be easy, but you know you must do it. You have to stop running.'

I was scared but I had a new-found strength.

I straightened my tie and we walked through the front doors together. I got to the front desk and was greeted by a young female desk clerk.

'How can I help you?'

I looked at Dad; he nodded for me to continue.

'I've come to hand myself in.'

'OK, and what is that for?' I think she thought I was a mad bloke.

'I'm an escaped prisoner from HMP Romwell.'

Her eyes opened wide, she looked flustered and worried. She'd not dealt with an enquiry like that before. She picked up the phone to call for help.

'Can I take your name please?' she asked.

'Sommers. David Sommers . . .'

A CON FORMERLY KNOWN
AS DAVEY

It would have been too hot and uncomfortable to wear clothes underneath. It was the same as any boiler suit really, only brightly coloured in LOUD green and yellow. That's what you have to wear when you're an E-Man. The privilege of ordinary prison clothes is no longer yours. Not that it's like having your Armani suit confiscated. But it is another small liberty taken away. Everywhere you go, and I do mean everywhere, you have to be escorted by a screw, and they have to get permission from Comms to move you. Even when you go down to get your dinner you have to have a screw holding your hand. Some of it is totally over the top, but I wasn't in a position to argue.

Since being banged up again, I'd had a lot of backlash, not just because I'd escaped but also because of who I used to be. I spent a lot of time in the Hospital Wing detoxing. It's not like I was 'cured' after that mysterious night but there is no denying I was different. I saw life as precious, it had meaning and what I'd done in the past was terrible. And I never had the mental need for drugs again. I didn't cluck like I used to. I had violent convulsions and fits instead because my body desperately wanted some of the poison I used to feed to it. The hospital staff were really good with me. They gave me several different types of medication to control my body and help rid me of those terrible symptoms.

The screams still haunted me at times. They would wake me from sleep, or catch me out when I was enjoying a moment's peace. It was as if they were waiting for me to relax, so they could pounce. I was given different forms of medication to suppress the screams. None of them worked. They just presented me with a different set of mind-altering problems. They would make me feel groggy or out of control. So I had to find my own way of controlling them. Instead of letting them control me, I would ride the storm. Step outside myself. And exercise was a huge help. I would literally sweat the voices quiet. Whenever they started, I would squat, burpee, press-up and crunch myself into oblivion. It was my way of taking control.

I had a lot of psychoanalysis, which led to diagnosis after diagnosis. Schizophrenia, drug-induced psychosis, personality disorder, severe depression, paranoia, bi-polar, BDD and a combination of all of them! And there were several medical terms they came up with to name the voices that I heard. I came to know them as the Opponent, the Self, the Enemy, the Temptation, the Ego – even the Devil or Satan. Whatever I called it, it was the badness that lurked inside me. It's the wrong in all of us. We all have it, only for a long time mine controlled who I was. What caused it? Was it the drugs, or had it always been there? That's a question I can't answer. It's a question that doesn't really need answering. It doesn't change the fact that I had it, I was that way and now I was trying to learn how to deal with my condition.

I couldn't find the answers in a medical book. I couldn't find the answers at the bottom of a pill box. I spent hours in my cell reading inspirational books, including the Bible. With my Dad's profession being what it was, I was familiar with the readings already. It was natural for me to spend time scrubbing up on the Christian faith. I was the son of a Christian pastor, after all. I spent hours, days, months in my cell, reading and learning. The whole dogmatic and sectarian point of view baffled me, though. The teaching that their path was the only path confused me. I found it biased and unjust, even within its own belief structure. The more I learned, the more I struggled to see any unity, or spirituality and connection with the essence of the universe. It made me uncomfortable with the idea of pigeonholing myself in a religion. I felt that my beliefs were unique to me. What is right for me may not be right for everyone. What is my truth, is not someone else's. I'm not the first prisoner to have found life answers from God, religion, spirituality or whatever you want to call it, and I won't be the last.

Even though I didn't find one religion that answered my needs, I still read, still prayed and I started to learn the benefits of meditation. That, along with my focus on fitness, saw me progress like I'd never done before. I started to come to terms with who I used to be. I repented – still do. I don't know if karma has served me all that I'm due, but I sure know that if it hasn't, it most certainly will.

I was starting to feel well. More learned – I was a sponge absorbing what I was reading.

Eventually I was moved to a normal wing, though I continued to be an E-Man. It had taken me a long time to get there, but there I was.

I put my suit on and waited, as I always did. My landing screw always knew what my day held, which was one good thing, I guess. Since Comms had to know where I was, I always turned up on time for things. Something that never usually happens inside.

It was a Sunday morning and I was going to attend the Sunday Service. Even though I didn't consider myself a Christian, I felt comfortable attending and praying there.

I'd already had a shave and wash but, once I was dressed,

I checked myself over – making sure I looked presentable and clean. I'd kept my hair clippered short and I shaved every day. My cell was immaculately clean. I had the floor highly polished, there wasn't a bit of dust in sight. The books and my belongings were all neatly stacked on my desk, or on the shelves I was provided with. Because I was an E-Man and, considering my previous history of extreme violence, I was single bang up, so it was easy to keep things tidy. My cell door opened and I was greeted by Mr Wise, smiling from ear to ear, as usual.

'Morning, Davey boy!'

'Hello, Guv, how you doing?' I was always pleased to see him. 'It's David now, if you don't mind!'

'Sorry, mate, keep forgetting you've squared all with him upstairs!' He put his hands to his chest, laughing.

Although it was nice to be addressed by my first name, I didn't like being called Davey anymore. I saw that as my former self. A person who no longer existed. I had moved on.

'You're a funny guy, Mr Wise. Maybe one day you'll know what I do, huh?' I winked and touched my nose.

'Either way, I suppose David is better than the Davey who smashed the fuck out of eight officers!'

'You got it, kid!' I laughed.

He radioed through to Comms to get permission to move me from the wing to the Chapel. As we moved, there were the usual 'All right, Davey' remarks. My former self still held some weight in the prison. There were people who were convinced I was just biding my time, waiting to explode, like I normally did. There were many people who didn't believe I had handed myself in. They thought it was all bullshit. That I must have been caught. Davey Sommers wouldn't have handed himself in. Davey this, Davey that. There were a lot of people who claimed to have been associated with me in the past. When people spoke of me or to me, they could have been friend or foe, for all I knew. I couldn't even begin to try and fathom who was and who wasn't. Living in a fog of drugs and violence does nothing for your attention to detail. I remember feelings and events but faces, people and former associates, they were a problem. That's why I kept myself to myself. I was never discourteous or silent, I just found it easier to be alone and concentrate on my studies. It's funny how things change. How things turn out. Being alone with my thoughts was the only thing I couldn't handle in my so-called heyday. But now, it was the main comfort I had. I could ride the screams and read a book. Learn and absorb.

The Chapel was situated in the hub of the prison. All wings grew off the hub. Prisoners were queuing at the ends of their wings, waiting to be counted in. I walked past them all. Being an E-Man, Comms needed to know when I left my original location and when I turned up at the new location. If I wasn't radioed in within a sensible time, the search parties would start coming. I never did find out what that sensible time was. Knowing the Prison Service, it was probably eight days!

I walked past everyone and into the Chapel. The Chapel orderly was already inside. He was a trusted prisoner, who worked there cleaning and doing odd jobs for the vicar. The band, made up of civilian helpers and prisoners, were inside, too, and a choir, made up of both as well. Nearly all the prisoners who were in the choir or band had 'found God'.

'Good morning, David,' said the vicar. Strong-willed and kind, he didn't take any shit from the cons. I say any shit, that's a slight exaggeration. But he wouldn't be shy about shouting at or banning the severely disruptive.

We shook hands.

'You had any more thoughts about joining the choir or the band?'

'That's very kind of you, but I don't think it would be appropriate.'

'Well, you know that it's always open to you.'

He always tried to get me involved with the Chapel, in any way he could. I didn't hide the fact that I didn't consider myself a Christian, and that I came to Chapel simply because I enjoyed his way of communion. He respected me for that. He knew I had a kind of relationship with the Divine, but that it wasn't strictly to any code. He allowed me to pray any way I saw fit. I think he was happy to have a prisoner in Chapel who had some sort of belief, however watered down. Unfortunately, Chapel was the best place to deal drugs, pass weapons and start riots, so not everyone in there was looking for spiritual enlightenment. The fact is that it's one place in prison where you have a load of cons from all the different wings mixed together. You'd get blokes smashed up by an enemy from another wing. The assailants would get bent up and then the service would continue normally. You could say it was quite different to the Sunday Service Dad used to take.

I took my seat at the back of the hall, like I did every week. I always wanted to be out of the way so I could listen, think, contemplate and pray. Mr Wise radioed through to Comms to say I was there.

'See you after, David.'

'Cheers, Mr Wise.'

As he left the Chapel, the inmates from all the other wings started to come in. They'd drag their heels, hugging and greeting each other. 'Yes, blood,' 'Blut blut!' Hugging and greeting each other were all ways to pass drugs.

I sat there in deep thought and the screws who manned the Chapel took their positions.

'When you digging out then, Sommers? Or is one of the Archangels coming down to fly you out of here, huh?'

It was common for me to get jibes from the screws. I'd made so many enemies and they couldn't forget my former self. They didn't care that I'd had years added to my sentence for my escape. They didn't care that I'd changed. They just saw it as either another plot, or as a weakness. I became accustomed to pot shots from these cowards who wouldn't have dared cross the old Davey. I made a choice not to fight, not to argue. I'm not going to say it was always easy, because it wasn't. Far from it. I wouldn't and will not allow myself to be attacked without defending myself but that was it.

I sat there and let him jibe. He was a good ten years younger than me and, by the looks of things, he had been a screw for about five minutes. He was showing off in front of his friends.

'Eight-man unlock? You're fuck all, mate. FUCK ALL.'

I looked up at him, straight in the eyes.

'Yeah, YEAH?' he said, stepping forward pretending to be ready to fight. Waiting for his mates to hold him back.

I looked forward and smiled to myself. Not outwardly, but inside. I knew he was a mug, an idiot full of bravado who was just trying to show how tough he was. Trying to exercise his power over me. Newsflash – the old Davey doesn't exist anymore. I had to expect it, though. I knew what I'd done. How I'd been. But through the sober eyes of my new conscience – through the eyes of David – I was shocked by all the kudos and fight my former self carried.

The Chapel was nearly full. I looked round and saw Tommo standing not too far away from me. He looked drugged up to his eyeballs. He'd obviously been taking loads of his own gear. He never used to do that. I clocked a meathead standing a few feet behind him. The new muscle. He must have been fifteen or twenty years my junior. A huge lump of a man who looked totally out of his nut. I could see him frowning at everyone who moved. He was aggressive, nasty and shoving people around. I didn't know who he was, but it was obvious the screws were all scared of him.

I tried to look away before I got eye contact with Tommo. Too late.

'Davey boy, how's it going, bruv?' He came walking towards me. It was the last thing I needed. 'It's been fucking ages, yeah. You OK over there on D Wing? You want me to hook you up?' He was loud, very loud.

'All right, Tommo, I'm good. Happy. Don't need anything, cheers. Look after yourself.'

I turned my back; I wanted to let him know the conversation was over.

'Hey, hey, don't turn your fucking back on me. Who the fuck do you think you are?'

I ignored him. People were beginning to notice. Cons and staff alike.

'I'm fucking talking to you!'

'You're out of your nut and I ain't interested. Step off,' I said, looking away.

'I said I'm talking to you.' He pushed my head hard.

I jumped up off my chair in a flash, twisting his wrist, dropping him to the floor in a second.

'Knew I'd get the chance to get you outta retirement, Davey Sommers. You're fuck all,' Tommo's muscle shouted.

He came plodding towards me. He carried a lot of weight in his midriff as well as his muscles. He was heavy, clumsy, but could obviously fight. I wasn't about to take any chances.

'Stop, we ain't gotta do this,' I said, putting my hands up.

Tommo was scrambling to his feet.

'Fuck him up!' he screamed to his man.

Everyone looked on intently. No screw was going to jump in. This was new versus old. But I wasn't the man they thought I was. I'd changed. Why couldn't they just let me be?

He got closer, almost on top of me. I saw him salivating at the mouth. His thick legs wobbled as he walked. The adrenaline was pumping through him. His fist clenched.

I knew what I had to do. I was clear-headed. I wasn't prepared to be hurt. No one was going to stop him. I had to do it.

He took an almighty great swing at me; I stepped to the left dodging it with precision. I cracked him clean on the jaw, throwing all my weight into it. BANG! He hit the floor and was fast asleep. Just like that. One punch. A subtle sigh filled the room. Disappointment. They wanted to see more violence. See a showdown. Have old Davey back. But he wasn't and never would be. That was the point.

The jibing screw came running at me like Robocop. I stood there placidly, Tommo was barely standing and the lump was snoring.

'Whoa, whoa, I'll walk to the Seg,' I said.

Even though I knew I'd done nothing wrong, I was pretty sure I would be walked there, searched and asked what had happened. I had a couple of hundred witnesses anyway.

He didn't listen, he pounced on me, trying to grab the back of my head and wrap me up.

'What you doing, you nutter? I'll walk!' I screamed, pushing him off.

I saw four more screws come charging. 'Oh, it's like that, is it?' I thought. They wanted to exercise their power. Show they could handle Davey. I did the only thing I could. I went placid. I let Robocop drop me. I went down without any resistance. He ended up on one of my wrists, bending it hard into a lock, causing me untold pain.

'ARGH!' I screamed, struggling involuntarily from the pain.

'Stop fucking moving,' he ordered, banging on more pain.

The more pain he applied, the more I involuntarily struggled. The screw on my other arm was OK, and the one who had control of my head was no bother. Just the show-off on my wrist.

I was eventually radioed through, and the Orderly Officer in charge came to attend. He could see that I wasn't struggling and wasn't offering any resistance, so he ordered the officers off me. He did have me walked to the Seg and strip searched, even though I pleaded my innocence. Seemed like no one wanted me to change.

I sat in the strip cell for about ten minutes, just staring at the dirty, stained walls. Awful memories came back of my sick-minded ferocity. I heard talking outside the cell. It was two members of staff.

'I don't give a fuck what that stupid cunt said he saw. I've known this man for more than eleven fucking years. He would not have started fuck all. I'm ending this charade right now and taking my prisoner.'

'There's rules and regulations, investigative procedures that need to be followed.'

'Don't give me that bollocks. If that were the case, you'd have stopped Tommo dealing and sorted out his muggy bit of brawn. But you ain't, so get the fuck outta my way.'

I heard the key force its way into the cell door. I jumped back. Mr Cramfield stood there facing me.

Since being on D Wing I'd come across him again. Only now he had highly polished Senior Officer pips on his shoulder. It was funny that he ended up in a senior position on my wing. We never really spoke at first, but now it was different. Civil. Sometimes on the brink of being friendly. A lot of years had passed. A lot of fights, sure. But we knew each other. The familiarity was difficult to ignore.

The Seg SO stood staring at Mr Cramfield.

'Thought I told you to piss off?' Cramfield said.

The Seg SO jogged on.

'Come on then, David . . . er, Sommers,' he quickly tried to cover himself. He never addressed anyone by their first name. Not in a million years.

'Yes, Guv,' I replied.

We walked out of the Seg and were clearly heading somewhere that wasn't the Chapel or the wing.

'Where we going, Guv?'

'I won't have any fucker messing with my cons for no reason.' He wasn't listening to me.

'I'd like to go to Chapel and catch the end of the service, if I can?'

'Takes the piss, Sommers. Don't get me wrong, we've had our ups and downs but, fuck me, you ain't bothered no cunt of late.' I smiled slightly at his ramblings. 'He can fuck his procedures, if some cunt tries to hit you, then you're entitled to defend yourself.'

We stopped dead and he faced me.

'He did try to hit you, didn't he?' He looked me deep in the eye.

'Yes, Guv, he did. I didn't want to fight. I don't even know why I got bent up.'

We started walking again.

'Good. Not good that someone tried to hit you or you got bent up. You know what I mean.'

We were quiet for a minute or so.

'Guv, can I ask you a question?'

'What?'

'Where are we going? I would really like to go back to Chapel.'

'They won't let ya go back now, not after that, not even if it's not your fault.'

I was confused. We were heading towards the Education Block, but Education wasn't open at the weekends.

'Where we going, then?'

'There's a bloke who works over here called Jonas. You know him?'

'No, can't say that I do.'

'You should meet him. Education would suit you down to the ground.'

'Problem with Education, Guv, is no one's there to learn. I'm through with drugs. I wanna keep my head down; learn the stuff I wanna learn. You know?' Like most places in jail, Education was a breeding ground for drug dealing, lazing about and bullying.

'Yeah, I do know. That's why I want you to meet this bloke Jonas. He teaches music, philosophy and all that stuff . . . Like, you know, you like,' he nodded as he said it.

'He's into spirits and the cosmos, is he?' I teased him.

Mr Cramfield looked a little embarrassed. 'Yeah, something like that.'

I laughed. 'You can have a bit of faith, Guv. It don't make you a wimp.'

'Suppose so. You're evidence of that!'

We shared a laugh.

'I appreciate it and all but, like I said, Education ain't worth going to, cos not much learning ever happens there. Besides, it's Sunday and, forgive me, Boss, but Education is shut.'

He tutted before going on, 'What do you take me for?'

'Should I answer that!?' I laughed.

'I know Education is shut, but Jonas sometimes comes in on a Sunday to prepare his lessons, play his fiddle, pray and all that other shit. He's here so I phoned him up, told him about you, and he said he'd be happy for you to go and have a chat with him.'

'He knows about everything I did?'

'Yeah but, like you fucking bleat on about, that was "Davey". You're no longer that man.' He cracked a smile and laughed.

We got to the Education Block at the back of C Wing. He unlocked the gate and sent me through.

'Right, he's in one of the classrooms. Not sure which one.'

'Guv, ain't you supposed to tell Comms where I am?'

'Never mind that bollocks, I'll tell them in my own good time. I know where you are, that's all that fucking matters.'

'Thank you, Guv.'

I held out my hand to shake his. He stared at me, then my hand. His guard slowly dropped as he reached out. Our hands gripped with a firmness and warmth that erased any past ills. We shook and looked at each other as we did so. Not so different, is what we were both thinking. We didn't need words to express that. It was a turning point. A moment that neither of us would forget.

'The name's Geoff. If you can't fucking call me that after all these years, then I'm some sort of cunt! I've spent more time rolling around with you than I have my missus and kids!'

We both laughed.

'Thanks, Geoff. I never thought we'd get to this. It's a funny old world.'

'Quick, get in there before I start believing your mumbo jumbo bollocks!'

I went in and he locked the gate behind me.

As I walked further inside, I heard music. It was blasting out. It wasn't any type of music I'd listened to before. It was classical – loud violins and orchestra.

'Jonas?' I called.

There were several classrooms off the main corridor. I didn't know which one he was in. I knew he was the only one there and I had nothing to worry about, but the loud music in an empty corridor was a little disconcerting.

'JONAS?' I shouted a little louder.

The music seemed to be reaching a climax. The violins shook, the bass fell deeper.

I yelled, 'JONAS ARE YOU . . .' The music stopped . . . 'THERE?' My voice echoed through the classrooms.

Within a second or two, an excitable man came running out. He carried more weight than he should have and was in his fifties, at a guess. Greek, Italian, Middle Eastern, I didn't have a clue. He wore trendy glasses, a checked shirt and corduroys. His hair was messy but fashionable, his shoes and trousers old fashioned. He was a perfect mix of 'with it' and 'past it'. Old and young. Nutty professor meets hip dad. He had a huge smile and was ridiculously excited.

'The Four Seasons, don't you just love it? The louder it's played, the more exquisite, don't you agree?'

'I can't say I know what it is.'

'What do you mean?' he said looking confused. No sooner had he said it, though, his smile became more professional and he started walking towards me with his hand held out.

'You must be David?'

We shook hands.

'Pleased to meet . . .' I didn't get a chance to finish my sentence.

'What do you mean you don't know what The Four Seasons is!?'

His smile returned as he slung his arm around my shoulders. A true eccentric. A man who appeared to have the proverbial ants in his pants. I felt a good aura from him straight away. We walked into the classroom and sat down.

'So, David Sommers, tell me something about yourself.'

I was a little taken aback but I answered calmly, 'Well, I'm a man who once thought he had everything and lost it. Then I came to prison and lost even more, if that was possible, including the best part of my mind. I escaped and realised that all I had lost were things I didn't need in the first place and things that had hindered my life. Since my return to prison, I've been studying and am slowly learning that what it is I'm now searching for and am beginning to find, makes me richer than I've ever been in the past.'

He stared at me with his jaw practically on the floor. 'Geoff was certainly right about you, wasn't he?'

'What do you mean?'

'That was spoken like a true philosopher. He told me that you used to be a downright maniac, and then something happened to you a year or two ago, which caused you to make a radical change to your life. The first words I hear from you and they are potent and thought-provoking. Amazing.'

I didn't know where to look. This man seemed so utterly at ease with himself in every way. He was flamboyant, but kind and clever. He felt free to offer me compliments. He didn't feel obliged to talk to me, or that it was a bind. He showed me sincerity and a genuine interest.

'What is it you do here exactly?' I asked.

He took his glasses off and rubbed his face as if it was a difficult question to answer. 'Well, I'm a teacher, of sorts. I teach all the basics from literacy to maths. It's a tough world out there without the basic skills.' I nodded. 'Since I've been here, though, I've started to do a lot more than just that. I teach music to those that WANT to learn it. I mentor guys that want to push themselves academically. I listen, I help, I mentor and guide in any way I can.'

'I thought that no one does sod all over here?'

'I'm not stupid or blind. There are guys who come to mark time, get out of their cell or deal drugs. I don't waste my time with those people. That's not my thing. There are plenty of staff over here who can deal with that; me, I work in a different way.'

'How?' I asked, becoming more and more interested.

'Well, you don't see any other members of staff here on a Sunday, do you!?' he laughed. 'I plan, I prep, I love doing what I do. That's me. But tell me about your experience – this change of heart.'

I started the story from the beginning. It was a rollercoaster of information; telling him about the ups and downs, the screams, the pain, the likes, the dislikes, the search for spiritual and eternal happiness. Not the usual tale from a dangerous villain. I spoke of my problems with organised religion, the books I'd read, the sense some of them made, the questions others posed. He listened intently and seemed interested in everything I was saying. This guy knew his stuff. He quoted philosophers, sages and mystics of the past. He knew the viewpoint of Abrahamic and Dharmic religions. He made sense.

'The questions that you're posing, the worries and contradictions you seem to see, are the same that I had, too, as do lots of people who search for answers in life.'

He passed me two books: the *Kitáb-i-Aqdas* and the *Kitáb-i-Íqán*. They were both authored by Bahá'u'lláh. I'd never heard of the books or the author.

'What are these?' I asked tentatively.

'Have you heard of the Bahá'í Faith?' he asked me.

'No, that one must have passed me by!' Not only had I not

heard of it, I was starting to think that perhaps Jonas's eccentricity was more than a character quirk. This felt one step too far.

'Read them both, cover to cover. I believe they may well help you.' He flipped back into excited mode, 'Now, what about music? What do you like? How about Bach? Such beautiful music!'

I struggled not to laugh. 'I'm more a Hendrix fan, or The Who to be honest. I'm into rock stars not stiffs in suits.'

He looked at me like I was mental. 'The art of beautiful music doesn't have to be expressed by stiffs in suits! Look.'

He pressed play on the video that he had been watching earlier. Out blasted Vivaldi. I nearly fell off my seat, it was so loud. Just as I was about to screw my face up, I saw a punk rocker playing the violin. It was Nigel Kennedy thrashing his instrument like a man possessed. I was captivated. Blown away by his sound, style and technique. I could feel the music, hear the emotion. Connect.

I stared at Jonas, watching him enjoy the music like a man who'd never heard it before. I listened, too. I looked at the master playing his instrument. I stared at the two books sitting on my lap. I clutched them tight. I felt a blanket of happiness cover me. More of the puzzle was beginning to fall into place . . .

DEPARTED

I was breathing heavily. Really heavily. I was doing my best to keep it as quiet as I could, though. I didn't want to wake Terry up at five in the morning.

It was my daily routine. A ritual, in many respects. I would rise at dawn, do an in-cell workout until I was well and truly awake, alert and in control. I was pushing out hundreds of press-ups and sit-ups with ease. It was a way of feeling clean and fresh. Free. My workout was made harder by having to hold my breath practically, so as not to disturb Terry.

It wasn't warm in our cell, so building up a sweat was a good thing. Your body heat can raise the temperature in the cell – sometimes it would make it stuffy and uncomfortable for your pad mate. That day, not a chance.

I'd become thin and toned. My body hardly carried any fat. I'd come to learn that I didn't need much food. Not that I starved myself. Not by a long shot. But I'd come to recognise that my normal portions of food only made me tired and sluggish. I would feel clouded and concentration would elude me and my focus would drift.

I ate as sensibly as I could. It's not exactly five-star food in prison, but you can still make sensible choices. I normally had cereal for breakfast, fruit for lunch and chicken and vegetables for dinner, sometimes with rice. I wouldn't buy anything from canteen, so I'd eat three times a day and only drink water, or perhaps a green tea if I could get hold of some. Miss Rogers used to drink it, so when she was on duty she would happily give me a few tea bags.

Mr Wise, Miss Rogers and Mr Cramfield all worked on D Wing. I came to know them as Jack, Jessica and Geoff. I became fond of all three of them. We had history. They had all done a lot to help me in their own ways. Sure, Geoff and I despised each other for the first decade or so, but eventually we learned a lot from each other. Geoff referred to it as a ten-year flirt!

I hammered out my last few press-ups and was starting to feel the satisfying muscle burn. The sweat dripped off my brow. Even though it was cold, I opened the window slightly, put my face to it and breathed in the fresh, cool air. I closed my eyes and let the icy fresh air cool my warm throat and fill my lungs. It felt good, refreshing. It gave me the chance to catch my breath, cool down and feel the alert and fulfilling burn of an exercised body.

I turned to check on Terry. He was still asleep.

I hadn't seen him for several years before he was transferred to my cell. He'd gone through the prison system for a while, before eventually being released. He went straight back on to the streets, though, taking copious amounts of drugs. He had ended up back inside; back at The Well.

They had taken him over to the Hospital Wing for some time to help him detox. It worked, which was amazing since he'd not been clean for years. Miss Rogers, who had been working over there at the time, noticed Terry was quieter than usual, which was quite something since he'd always been a man of few words. She was concerned about him, so she put him on self-harm watch. When she was transferred to D Wing, she decided to have him transferred there, too, so she could keep an eye on him. She had him put in a cell with me because she thought another familiar face would be good for him. I instantly recognised a tortured man. Someone who wanted to forget. Not to feel; but to sleep. This is why he'd spent so much of his life out of his mind on drugs. The funny thing is, all the other times he'd been in prison, he'd never been given detox. It wasn't like he refused it, he'd just never been offered it and he'd gone with the flow, and his flow was taking drugs.

When he was first brought over, he seemed pleased that he was going to double up with me. Strange really, since back in the day all I did was bully him. It took me ages to convince him I was different. He found it quite funny at first. He thought it was another of my plans. Another scam to escape, or something. Eventually, though, I convinced him. I first made peace with him, apologising profusely for how I'd treated him. Like everything else about me, he found that difficult to swallow. I also told him about my faith. I never preached to him. That's not what I do. I'm not some know-it-all guru who shoves it down everyone's throats. I am just someone who follows a particular way. A way that works for me.

Terry and I spent hours together, doing what we all do best inside: talking. More importantly, this time I listened. I'm not going to say I got a flurry of information from him all in one go, because that wasn't Terry's way. But he did open up. I found out that he had spent his life in care homes. He never knew his father and only met his mother a few times when he was growing up. She was an alcoholic and drug addict. He had no biological siblings that he was aware of. And he told me about a foster brother he lived with for a number of years. How this foster brother used to force-feed Terry drugs, bully, beat and habitually rape him.

It didn't take a genius to work out Terry's savage past had had a huge impact on his life. He had withdrawn from living an alert life. For a while, he did self harm. He didn't do it in a way that was visible to others, though. He didn't, like some self harmers, wear his wounds visibly, as a cry for help. But sharing a cell with him allowed me to see his bare chest and legs. Where there weren't cuts, there were burns.

When he eventually stopped, he started to display outward signs of being a happier person. It seemed to me that he was beginning to cope a lot better. He didn't become an extrovert, or anything like that, but he started to show a little interest in life.

I watched him snoring away looking content. Peaceful. I had to keep an eye on him around some of the other lads as he was a target for bullies. He'd not grown the confidence to deal with them. He didn't have the courage to stand his ground, however that manifested itself – force of words, or force of action.

I took my clothes off and had an in-cell wash with soap and water. A clean body and clean living space were just as important to me as a clean spirituality. One goes hand in hand with the other.

Once that was done, I put on some clean clothes. There was kit change every week, which I attended, of course, but I also cleaned my clothes during the week. I washed them in the sink and dried them in the cell. I had a shave and final freshen up.

I then read quietly from my *Kitáb-i-Aqdas* and spent some time meditating. I'd become a follower of the Bahá'í Faith – a nineteenth-century religion, it came out of Persia and was founded by Bahá'u'lláh. The basic principles are that there is one God, the creator of everything, and that this world has been created for us to attain spiritual growth and knowledge. It promotes spiritual unity for all humankind. It teaches that, over time, the world has been sent divine messengers – Krishna, Abraham, Buddha, Jesus, Mohammed and most recently Bahá'u'lláh. He calls these prophets (including himself) manifestations of God and explains that all their messages are good and correct, and that they constitute the best rules and divine laws of the time. None is the one and only truth, and none is wrong. As much as the Bahá'í Faith has ideas, rules and regulations on morals and issues of law, it also promotes a mystical connection between us and the Divine. It is a non-violent belief system, which denounces any form of fighting in the name of religion.

Bahá'u'lláh wrote the *Kitáb-i-Aqdas* (The Most Holy Book) and the *Kitáb-i-Íqán* (The Book of Certitude), as the two most important texts of his newfound religion. They were the two books that Jonas had given to me. When I had first read them, they made sense and answered a lot of the questions I had been struggling with.

I sat and meditated as Terry slept on. When I finished I felt invigorated and ready for the day, and Terry was just getting out of bed.

'Instead of just sitting there, whack the kettle on,' he said.

Our kettle was a new bit of kit – every cell had one.

'You ready for football this morning?' I asked.

His face was still creased from sleep. 'Yeah, can't wait!' he said, sarcastically.

I jabbed him playfully in the arm. 'Where's your spirit, huh?'

'Still fast asleep!'

I made us a brew and we chatted over our bowls of cereal. We could hear the screws turning up for their day's work. The familiar noises of the fellas shouting out the windows at each other began. The odd door was heard being unlocked, as some guys were shipped out to court.

I felt happier than I had in years. I broke my days up into segments. I always had an activity to do. Something that would keep me busy, interested and focused. It was all about learning. My personal development was my new bird killer.

Terry seemed in fairly decent spirits. Tired and a little ratty at first, but then he never was an early riser. He had a quick wash and got his gym stuff together. The PEIs had turned up on the wing to collect the cons who were playing indoor football.

We played five-a-side in the mornings twice a week. I also managed to go to the gym and weights room pretty often since I was an 'enhanced prisoner'. It's a simple equation, you're well behaved and you get privileges. You're not and you'll get sweet FA.

I was bouncing up and down, looking forward to football. 'How the fuck do you do all that shit in the morning, then have the energy to play football?' Terry asked me, half smiling.

'It's all in the mind, Terry boy. The body does what the mind tells it to. You've just got to take control of your mind first!'

The door unlocked, Terry and I sprang out on to the landing.

'Morning, gentlemen,' said Miss Rogers.

'Morning, Miss,' I said.

'What's wrong with him?' she asked, pointing to Terry.

'He's not a morning person, are ya, mate!'

He just smiled.

'You two behave over there – play nicely and all that!'

She carried on about her business as we made our way downstairs to wait for the PEI. He had a list of all the cons he wanted – he would unlock the doors and it was our responsibility to get down to the Ones and wait for him, in good time. It was a privilege to play sport and go to the gym. The gym screws didn't want to waste their time dragging you out of bed. If you didn't make the effort, your name would be crossed off and you wouldn't go again.

We were one of the first downstairs. I always made sure of that. By the time the PEI was back on the Ones, all of us were ready and waiting. It's the one and only time a con will do his hardest to be on time. It was a pleasure, going to the gym.

The prison was remarkably quiet. Morning exercise

hadn't begun, so it was a fairly quiet time – except for the lads kicking their doors and screaming for a screw to attend their cell. There were also a few cons making their way to reception, clutching their worldly belongings in plastic prison bags. They were either going to court, being ghosted to another prison or perhaps being released. You could normally tell by the looks on their faces.

We made our way across the centre to C Wing. The gymnasium was situated up on the Fours at the back of the wing, over Education but a level lower. There were twelve of us in total – five-a-side and two on the bench. We would rotate.

The PEI warmed us up until a few blokes looked as though they were going to be sick. I was loving it. We broke up into two teams and the fun began. It was good football; we all got stuck in and let ourselves go. I wasn't that good, but my level of fitness ensured that I didn't do too badly. As it was indoors and the pace was fast, you didn't really have to excel with masterful skills. Terry was gifted, though, even in that little arena.

We were playing for some time when the gate opened. As it did so, the ball was fired at the guy who walked in, just missing his head. Jonas. Everyone laughed, including Jonas. The game continued as I went over to him. I knew it was me he'd come to see.

'Morning, Jonas, how you doing?'

We shook hands.

'Great thanks. You're looking trimmer than ever; wish I could say the same for me,' he said, rubbing his portly stomach.

'You will eat those Danish pastries!'

He smiled.

'I've popped up here as it's pretty empty downstairs and we could have a practice together?'

'Would love to, but it's footy.'

'OK, just thought it would be a good time to have a go.'

I called over to the PEI.

'Guv, do you mind if I shoot downstairs with Jonas? He's offered to give me a quick lesson.'

'I ain't got a problem with that, way you go.'

I looked over to Terry, made sure he was OK, then we left the gymnasium and headed downstairs. As we walked into the Education Block, there were a few members of staff roaming around, preparing for the day. The cleaner, Reg, was there. He'd been a con at The Well for a thousand years.

'Morning, David,' he said, as he limped past barely able to hold his broom.

'What's happening, Reg, you all right?'

'Not too bad, just a hundred years short of being a free man!' Same comment every day.

I followed Jonas into his classroom. We went to the back where there were two violins. I smiled to myself, excited at the prospect of picking it up and playing.

Since that first time I had met Jonas, I found myself

mesmerised by the sound a violin could make. I spent years with Jonas, talking philosophy and learning to play the violin. I found it difficult, almost embarrassing at first. I watched the Nigel Kennedy video intently, totally blown away by his style, his look and the emotion in his playing. It seemed incredible to me that something so small and fragile had the capacity to create such a sensational sound. I went through several of his works with Jonas. He'd even managed to rework some of my beloved Jimi Hendrix.

Jonas and I picked up our violins. He pressed play on the CD player. A backing track came on – Vivaldi's Winter 1. It is a complex piece.

I listened intently and waited for my cue. As always, the last thing I looked at was Jonas's smiling, chubby face holding his violin, before I closed my eyes to concentrate fully. Each different part of the string section fired up, one after the other. The subtle jumps of the pumping music slowly began to speed up. I placed my bow on the strings and thundered through the teasing first solo. Louder, faster, quicker, the instruments went. Faster I pushed and pulled. Faster and louder the different sections went. My solo took the lead. Louder, louder. YES. Back in. Fast. Powerful. Climax. Close. Relax.

I opened my eyes to see the classroom filled with other members of staff who had heard us playing. One by one they had filtered in, unbeknown to me. I saw Jonas standing opposite me with his violin held by his side. He'd stopped to watch, as well, as I pushed myself harder than ever before.

I put down my violin and began to put it in its case. The room was totally silent. Then they all began to clap. Jonas put his arm around me.

'Now that's how you play the violin,' he said.

'It wasn't too fast?'

'It was magnificent.'

I was embarrassed. I'd never played in front of anyone before. There were several congratulations. I nodded slightly and sat on a stool, waiting for them to go.

'Why are you so embarrassed?' Jonas asked me.

'It's always been for me, you know. Not about showing off.' I'd considered the violin a personal thing. Just like my faith.

'David, you should be proud of how well you can play. It is a gift.'

I'd never looked at it like that.

'I best get back to the gymnasium now to grab a shower before it's time to head back to the wing.'

I walked into the gymnasium. All the blokes were in the showers. Footy had finished. I was hoping to have caught the last five minutes or so. I walked to the back of the hall, towards the changing room. The PEI was sitting in his office next door, having a brew.

'Grab a shower, Sommers, then I'll be getting you lot back.'

'Yes, Guv.'

I walked into the showers to see two blokes setting about Terry.

'You fucking wanker, think you're it out there.'

One of them punched him in the gut, the other in the back of the head.

'Oi!' I screamed. I ran into them, smashing them both out the way. 'The hell you doing?' I screamed at them. 'You all right, Tel?'

'Yeah, they just can't stand it that they're shit at football.'

'Come on!' one of them screamed, trying to get at Terry.

I shoved him back hard in the chest.

'Get back or you'll regret it,' I barked.

'Regret what?' shouted the other one. 'Davey Sommers is gone, is all we ever hear from you.'

I stepped in closer, getting into their personal space. They flinched; I didn't take my eyes off either one.

'Yeah, well you two might just get him out of retirement.'

They withered like poisoned weeds.

'You sure you're all right?' I asked Terry once more.

'Sweet.'

That was prison life, one minute you could have the most amazing experience of your life, the next you could be fighting for your life, or someone else's. You can never underestimate your surroundings. Prison is a ticking bomb. Through the day people get by with camaraderie and piss taking, but every situation has the potential to turn nasty.

That's why you've got to keep your wits about you if you're going to survive. Although I'd changed, I hadn't become a naïve prison idiot. I was developing my faith, but I hadn't become green to the horrific possibilities that each and every one of us faced. I knew only too well what people were capable of. I still had my memories. I knew what I used to be like and how I used to handle situations. How I handled people. I knew that there were hundreds of cons behind the door who were just as bad as I used to be. You had to keep your eyes open at all times. I knew that.

We finished our showers and waited by the door for the PEI to get off his arse. He eventually peeled himself off the chair.

'Everyone ready?' he asked, looking half asleep.

He unlocked the door and led us through to C Wing. They were all out on association. We rifled through the masses, saying hello to the blokes we knew.

'Terry, lad?' shouted some fella. He was a heavy-looking bloke, covered in tattoos, with a totally bald head. He didn't look the friendliest guy I'd ever seen. He was most definitely 'a face', judging by the company he kept. 'Terry, you ignorant little cunt?' he said a bit more aggressively.

Terry went white. Looked uncomfortable. Scared. I'd never seen him look so bad before. He hurried across the centre, back to home sweet home, and I followed him.

'Who the hell was that?' I asked.

He didn't answer me, just stared vacantly into the abyss.

'Terry, who was that? You look like you seen a bloody ghost!'

'Yeah, you're right there, I have. That fat fucking pig is Marshal.'

My jaw hit the ground. I couldn't believe what he was telling me. The stuff I learned about Terry – the violence, drugs and abuse. The rape. Marshal was the foster brother that had raped him.

I followed Terry back up to our cell. We stood by the door, waiting for a screw to unlock it.

'Hey, boys, what's happening?' Mr Wise was always cheerful.

Neither of us spoke.

'Fuck is wrong with you two moody bastards?'

'Not today, Jack,' I said.

He let it go and unlocked the door. Terry walked in and threw himself on his bed. I stood there, not really knowing what to say.

'There anything I can do, mate?' I asked.

He didn't say anything.

'Terry? Tel mate, look, we gotta talk about this. How you feel?'

'HOW DO I FUCKING FEEL? WHAT DO YOU THINK, HUH?' he screamed. He put his head back on his pillow. 'I don't want to talk, I just want to sleep.'

'I'm worried about you, mucker.'

He looked up at me, 'Seriously, David, I'm fine. Honest,

I'm fine. I just ain't seen him in years. It repulsed me, seeing him standing there full of bravado, full of bollocks. Just like he used to. Jack the fucking lad. A face. A hard nut. What they don't all know, though, is that he's a fucking nonce. A dirty, raping kiddie fiddler. It's hard for me. I just wanna get my nut down.'

'Fair enough, bruv. You need me, you know where I am, though.'

I continued about my business, keeping an eye on him. He seemed all right; a little more reclusive, but nothing compared to what he had been when he'd first arrived on the wing. I couldn't imagine what he had gone through, or how he felt. Seeing Marshal again banged up in the same prison, must have been hell.

We had our evening meal and sowsh and were banged up for the night. I went through my normal routine of reading, praying and meditating.

Terry and I played cards or chess most evenings. It was a good bird killer. That night Terry was pretty chatty. A lot more than usual.

'Sorry about earlier. It is just hard, ya know?'

'No worries, mate. I know it must be. I can't even imagine . . . That's why I want to be here to help, if I can. Jessica can hook you up with someone to talk to as well, if you want?'

He laughed and lit a cigarette, 'I don't need that, mate. I deal with things my own way.'

'Anyway you want, mate,' I said.

'You've become a good friend. Not saying you weren't before, but it was different.'

'I was a bully. I'm sorry.' I held my head in shame.

'You ain't got to apologise every time for that. I weren't no angel. We did have some funny times, with one thing in common, the drugs. This time, mate, you've been mega. I mean a really decent bloke. I know I don't say much, I know it appears I don't notice things, but I do. And I want to say thanks for making it all a bit easier this time round.'

There was a short silence.

'Enough of the appreciation society, you'll make me blush!' I said, pretending to punch him.

For the rest of the evening we chatted and laughed. In fact, I think Terry opened up to me more that night, than ever before.

I didn't need an alarm clock. I woke up instinctively shortly before five. I always did. I normally went to sleep just after midnight. Four and a bit hours was all I ever needed.

I sprang out of bed. It was still dark. Once on my feet I did a couple of stretches to wake myself up. I rubbed my eyes and waited for them to become adjusted to the light.

I looked at Terry's bunk. He wasn't in it. He wasn't in his bed. I didn't register at first. I looked around the cell in slow motion until I came to the window.

'GOD PLEASE, NO!' I screamed.

There he was, hanging from a ligature, made from his bed sheets. Although it was dark, I could see the colour of his cheeks. Grey stone. His lips were an off blue.

'AAARRRGGGHHH!' I screamed.

I pressed the cell bell and kicked the door with all my might.

'GUV, GUV, GUV, GET IN HERE! HE'S DYING. GUV PLEASE, GET IN HERE!' I screamed at the top of my voice. The night man was on duty. It's minimal staff when everyone's sleeping so I knew it could be longer than normal to get a response.

I ran to Terry's body, lifting him up to take his weight off the noose. He felt cold and wet. Saliva and blood seeped out of his mouth.

'Terry, lad, wake up. WAKE UP!' I screamed.

As his weight was lifted off the noose, his bowels and bladder emptied all down us both.

'WAKE UP, WAKE UP . . . GUV, PLEASE GUV, HURRY!' I was starting to cry.

I heard the cell door crash open. The night orderly came running in.

'Fuck, I'm coming,' he shouted.

He pulled out a fish knife and cut the ligature. We laid Terry down on his back. The orderly radioed through to the Hospital Wing and called for an ambulance. I knew, though, that he'd already gone.

I looked down at his cold body, dead on the cell floor; his

face, for the first time, looked as though it felt no pain. I wiped my tears away.

All the medics began to arrive.

'Let's get you out of here, son,' said the orderly.

I walked slowly backwards, staring at Terry as I did. It was TOO painful. He meant more to me than I ever realised.

'You rest now, Tel. You rest . . .'

THE COLOUR RED
(DON'T LOOK)

It was pretty noisy and hot in there but I still went over. You didn't get out of your cell much at weekends. There was no sowsh – instead, we were taken over to what is best described as a games room. We went over a couple of landings at a time. There was table tennis, pool, TVs, phones and showers. It wasn't that big so it could get blisteringly hot. Time in the games room coincided with kit change. If you refused your turn over there, you could kiss your clean clothes and bedding goodbye. I never missed it, even though it was hardly stimulating sitting over there with a load of geezers taking gear and gobbing off at each other. I was growing tired of prison. I was ready to leave. I didn't have that long left. Well, not long compared to how much time I'd already done. I was focusing on that. Jonas had left the jail. He'd taken a high-powered job at a University up north. We wrote to each other regularly, though. I used to love getting his letters. Eccentric and manic, but full of humour and wisdom. I was glad he found the time to keep up our correspondence – it helped me get me through the low points.

I wasn't slipping back into my old habits. But I was tired of the regime, the system and those who resided in it. Compared to when I'd first been locked up, prison was getting more out of control. It didn't use to be a walk in the park. I lived in a war zone in those early days – mostly of my own doing. But, generally speaking, the screws seemed to have a bit more control, back in the day. Yes, there were some useless cowards that wore the uniform. But the Prison Service was changing. They seemed to be trying to eradicate the bully boy tactics. They had partly achieved it. Not through and through – you'll never get that totally absolved in prison, or anywhere else for that matter. Bullies will always exist. That's an unfortunate part of everyday life. But it seemed to have gone the other way. Where staff used to strike first, deal with it later, they would now do nothing. The cons had no respect for them. In all honesty, they were like kids in uniforms, most of them. You still had Jack, Geoff and Jessica roaming the jail but the older, more experienced, staff seemed to be retiring, and being replaced with inept kids who had no strength of character or control. It wasn't really their fault. They were getting taught inadequate skills to deal with dangerous men. The place was running wild.

I wasn't the only one who felt it – most of the old lags did. We had become used to the rules and regulations. We knew where we stood. We understood the rules of the game. But the new fuzzy way of doing things made life inside confusing and inconsistent. You'd get a different answer from each screw every time you asked, even about the most basic requirements.

The new breed of prisoner had changed, as well. I'm not saying that respect and honour was always in the forefront of my mind when I was a crook – if that had been the case, I wouldn't have been a crook – but there were some unspoken rules. Older people, women and kids were left alone, for instance. But female officers were taking as many punches as the males, and pensioners (staff and con) were set upon by guys in their twenties.

Crime has no loyalty, but it seems it was more ruthless than ever. More than I ever remember it being. Maybe that's right, maybe not. Perhaps I'd just got older and more exhausted by the whole lifestyle.

I watched the other cons in the games room and listened.

'Fucking pussyhole, I'll cut him, blood. Carve him up for breakfast.'

'What about ya mother?' said his mate.

'Fuck her as well, innit.'

He was talking about his own brother. Taking him out. The white ball came bouncing off the pool table where they were playing.

'Pass the ball, pops,' he said to me.

I held his stare for a second and smiled, before bending down to pick it up for him.

'Yeah, sweet, pops,' he said as I gave it back to him.

It annoyed me. I didn't like his attitude. I wanted to slap him. Teach him a thing or two about life. He knew nothing about me, what I did, how I had changed and where I was going. I'd been feeling a lot of this anger. I was able to control it, but at times it was difficult. I got annoyed about the smallest of things. Like being called pops. The legend of Davey Sommers was slowly dying out. The young kids didn't know how mad I used to be. That's how I liked it – I didn't want to talk about my past. Not unless it was used to give a young guy some advice. But I still didn't like their attitude.

Since Terry died, I stayed as single bang up. They let me because my behaviour was good and also because I'd been inside for so many years. The screws thought I'd earned it.

I had spent so much time with Terry – listening, talking, making things better. Or so I thought. I was so upset when he died. Really, really knocked down by it.

It's not my call to decide if suicide is right or wrong. Terry's journey was personal to him. Perhaps he found his enlightenment. But my blood would boil when I'd think about Marshal and what he did to him. If I was ever going to slip back into Davey mode, I believe he would have been a trigger for it. The worst thing was he was now residing on D Wing. He took pleasure in staring at me, grinning. I think he knew that I knew his dirty little secret, and that I wouldn't do anything. Believe me, it was bloody difficult at times. I would find myself fantasising about hurting him. Thoughts would pop into my head; the old voice would start to whisper. Before it took hold, though, I'd exercise, pray and meditate. That would bring me back to reality. It was my way of keeping control.

I decided to go for a shower to kill some time and to get out of the games room. I stood up and looked around at everyone. The young screws were sitting at the side, not paying attention and mostly looking intimidated by the job they were supposed to be doing. I picked up my towel and walked slowly over to the showers. I put my hand out to push open the door. Suddenly Marshal jumped in front of me.

'He asked for it, you know. Dirty, little cunt,' he said grinning from ear to ear.

No one else could hear him. I stared into space, not wanting to be drawn into conversation or into a confrontation.

'He was put into homes especially for blokes like me; that's fact.' I gritted my teeth and stared away from him, switching off. 'I know you, Davey boy. I know what you and him used to get up to in that cell. First on A Wing, then over here.' He was enjoying being able to goad me. 'You can pretend all you want, but you and I know he done himself in cos you wouldn't leave him alone,' he said licking his lips. My heart rate went through the roof, my legs started to shake. My body was filling with adrenaline. 'Admit it, you like chickens, as well. You can pray all you want, but I know you do.'

I looked at him now. Straight in the eyes. He was grinning, laughing. He was staring at me. My lip started to curl, my fist clenched.

'You took over where I left off, didn't you? Don't worry about that piece of shit. There's lots more like Terry.' He pointed over to a really young-looking con. He seemed too young to be banged up. He looked scared for his life.

My breathing had become forced. My brow began to dampen. HIT THE CUNT HIT THE CUNT HIT THE CUNT. The voice turned into a scream. My ferocity came flooding back. I didn't want to stop it. I didn't want to let that pig get away. I clenched my fist tighter. I was ready. READY.

'You . . . You f . . .' I was struggling to contain it.

'You f-ing what?' he goaded. 'Go on, I fucking dare you, you washed-up cunt,' he turned aggressive. He was ready for a fight, as well. He was big man who feared no one. I pulled my fist back. My knee was shaking. KILL KILL KILL . . .

'GUV!' I screamed. 'Take me back to the wing.'

I was back to reality. I had managed to get a grip of myself. Stop myself from losing it.

The young screw came walking over.

'You FUCKING COWARD!' Marshal screamed, open palm slamming me hard in the chest. He knocked me flying. 'Come on!' He was desperate now.

'You'll get yours, Marshal. One day you'll be dealt with,' I turned and walked away with the officer.

I lay in bed, half asleep. It was early for me to be nodding off but my encounter with Marshal had drained me of a lot of my energy. I heard the keys jam into my cell door and turn. It woke me instantly. I jumped out of bed to be faced with Robocop. Over the years, he had built a reputation for bending people up for no reason and for being too heavy-handed. Robocop was a bully, pure and simple. A pig. An animal who hid behind the shirt.

'Can I help you, Guv?'

'You can start by talking to me properly, not like a fucking vicar, or summit.'

I noticed two screws standing by the door. Young and impressionable.

'What is it you want?' I tried to keep my manners. I had an idea which way this was heading.

'Where's the weapon?'

'What are you talking about?'

He stepped closer to me. I could sense he was ready for a fight. I didn't need it.

'Guv, I have not got a clue what you're talking about.'

'Don't fucking play innocent with me. Once a wrong'un, always a wrong'un. Marshal was done. You know it, I know it, so give me the fucking weapon?' He stepped even closer.

'Watch yourself, Guv, it ain't gotta go like this.'

Robocop was getting ready to use force. I'd seen it a thousand times.

'Sounds like the threat you gave Marshal earlier. You say that, then we find him hacked up like a bit of meat and now everyone knows he's a nonce. Funny that. So stop playing fucking games and give me the weapon.'

I didn't want to fight but I can't say I was sorry he had been hurt. Apparently Marshal had been banged up for raping his girlfriend's son. Not the armed robbery he'd told everyone. It had got out. But not from me. I hadn't even known that's what he was in for. Karmic law works when it chooses to. Somehow, someway you're dealt with. I believe Marshal was being served some deserved retribution.

Our altercation hadn't gone unnoticed, though, and Robocop put two and two together and made five. He wanted to be the one to bring me down. He'd found me guilty before he'd even unlocked my cell door. Having two screws behind him told me that.

'You're barking up the wrong . . .' I didn't have the chance to finish.

'YEAH?' He punched me in the temple, hard.

I didn't see it coming. BANG! And again. No way was I taking that. I smashed him hard in the ribs; instinct took over and I head-butted him in the nose. He fell back.

'ARGH!' he yelped.

The two other screws came running in and jumped on me.

'GET OFF ME!' I screamed.

I wasn't going to let them touch me. No way. I didn't deserve it. I punched, kicked and struggled with everything I had. I was still in control, though – it was me, not the enemy. I didn't deserve it, and I wasn't going to stand there and take it.

One of them managed to blow his whistle, which alerted the rest of the staff. Punches, elbows and kicks. One after the other, I dished them out. They couldn't get hold of me. My leaner, faster self was too quick for them. Too straight. I wasn't going to have it.

Two more screws ran into the cell, also diving on me. Again, I wouldn't allow it. I fought. I fought with all my might. Eventually, they got the better of me, though. There were too many of them. They got me to the ground.

'I'VE NOT DONE ANYTHING WRONG!' I screamed.

They cuff carried me all the way to the Seg.

I had a gown on and nothing else. I hadn't complied with the strip search. I felt it was unjust. I was being mistreated. I didn't deserve it.

Although I'd calmed down, I was still furious with Robocop's actions. It's one thing dealing with someone who needs to be dealt with but it's something else entirely being heavy-handed for no reason.

The cell door opened. I didn't bother to get up. I couldn't see the point in showing respect to someone when I didn't feel I had been treated justly.

'Haven't you grown too old for this?' It was a voice I recognised.

I looked up and saw Mr Stone – the screw who had signed me in at reception when I'd first been banged up. I'd not seen him in years. He had transferred years before. I thought he'd have long since retired. 'Mr Stone, what you doing here?'

'They let me do my last eighteen months back here as a governor.'

'It's funny seeing you in a suit!'

We laughed.

'First day back and I'm dealing with Mr Sommers who's been bent up. Sounds familiar, I thought. But I'd heard you'd changed. I'd heard good things about you.'

'Guv, look, I've not had a row in years. YEARS. I'm not the bloke you used to know. I didn't do anything to Marshal. NOTHING.'

He looked confused. 'I ain't worried about that nonce; looks as though he had it coming. I'm talking about assaulting an officer who asked you to turn your radio down.'

I laughed. I couldn't stop, 'That what he told you? Do I

really need to be messing about like that, this close to the end? Do you really believe I did that?' I looked at him deep in the eyes.

'Maybe not. What happened?'

'He's a bully, that's what happened. No point talking about it,' I said, waving my hands. I didn't see the point in taking it any further. Any decisions were normally made well before it went to adjudication. Plus Robocop's nose had been broken.

'It's not like it used to be, David. You wanna make a complaint; I'll see to it personally that it's followed through.'

I looked up at him and thought for a second. I wasn't in the business of having a man lose his job. But I also wouldn't tolerate being hit for no reason. It rushed through my mind how many vulnerable guys that bully had probably taken on. He had thought I was past it. If it hadn't been for that, he would have left me alone. He'd got the shock of his life when he took me on.

'OK, Mr Stone, I'll tell you what happened . . .'

F.E.A.R.

I put on the last clean tracksuit I had. I exercised, read, spent some time meditating and washed, like I did every day. As I got dressed, I went to the mirror to have a shave and check myself over for the last time. My cell was more immaculate than I'd ever had it. It looked naked. Everything that I didn't need, I had either given away or thrown in the bin. As I lived extremely modestly anyway, even for a prisoner, there wasn't that much to get rid of. The belongings I did want to keep were a few select books, pictures, pieces of music and letters.

My day had come. I was about to be released from prison. I'd dreamt about it, thought, contemplated and imagined my new life outside the four walls and the day had finally arrived.

I'd had a couple of day releases. It was a part and parcel of my reintroduction to society. I could have had some time with my family, but I opted out of that. I didn't want to make my final days any harder than they had to be. Seeing them and then having to go back inside would have been too difficult. Instead, I chose modest day visits to places nearby with a member of staff.

I'd had as many worries as I had happy thoughts. I was scared that I'd become institutionalised. My mind was free, so I was free, but I was worried how things would be on the outside. I'd changed, the world had changed. How was I going to cope? Was I going to be able to work in the field I wanted to work in?

I had had plenty of time to think. My final few months were marred slightly by the Robocop incident and investigation. Mr Stone was a man of his word, though. He put forward a full investigation about what had happened. One of the young officers, who had been standing at my cell door, admitted he heard the taunts and saw Robocop strike me. It seemed he didn't want me to be severely dealt with over something I hadn't done. It turned out he had a conscience.

Robocop, however, didn't. It came to light that he had assaulted dozens of inmates. One after another, the complaints came in. The prison wanted to pursue a criminal investigation at first, but I wasn't interested in doing that. I refused to go forward with it. All of the other cases had less evidence, were more circumstantial. But the picture had been painted and the service knew exactly what type of cowardly bully he was. So they sacked him. He got his just deserts. Karma was served, right where it hurt him. The punishment might not seem severe enough but, believe me, it was the end of his world when it happened. His job was his life. His life was the job. After being dismissed, I doubt he could even find employment as car park security.

After that was over, I really was just marking time. Clock watching.

I had plans for what I wanted to do when I got out. How I wanted to live and support myself. I was determined to achieve my goals. I could see the possibilities but the closer my release date got, the more anxious I felt. I started to see the old Davey. Not feel like him, just see him. I would see the worthless ex-con. A junkie. Society's scum. Would I be taken seriously? Would anybody want to associate with me?

All of those thoughts rushed through my mind. Dad and Adam knew what I wanted to do and they believed in me. Ever since I had handed myself in, Dad had been amazing. He could see that the Bahá'í Faith worked for me and that I'd become a man at peace. He didn't let his faith get in the way of supporting me. He was a liberal and wise man.

I'd spoken to Adam's children, on the phone and in letters. I'd built good relationships with them, as I had with his wife. I would write to them all individually and they all wrote back. It was wonderful – really uplifting. I never let them come to visit me, though – I didn't want them to associate me with prison. It wasn't a place for kind, innocent and impressionable minds. It was full of dangerous men. I didn't need them to see me in a place like that, even if I couldn't hide the fact that I was there. I'd tell them stories and answer any questions they had but I wouldn't let them visit me. I believed that I could get to know them through written words and on the phone. I believed that it would make my relationship with them that much richer, once I was eventually released. Now I was going to find out if I was right to do so.

I'd seen Adam and Dad three or four times a year. That's all I wanted. Because they had already seen me inside, I allowed us to share visits sometimes. The problem was I used to feel absolutely awful afterwards. It would make the subsequent weeks a real struggle. But after a few months, it would get to the point where it seemed worth the upset, just so we could see each other.

I was sitting in my cell, packed and nervous. I rubbed my cold and numb hands together. I felt the hairs on my body standing to attention, as goose bumps washed over me. This was it. Really it.

The noise in the jail was nearly at full volume. Doors were being kicked; the screams out of the windows were ferocious.

I could hear screws shouting and their heavy steps as they pounded the landings. I sat there, thinking deeply. Seventeen years I'd spent in prison. For seventeen years I'd heard that noise and been a part of that regime. It was difficult to believe that I'd never hear it again. It's not that I was going to miss it but, when something becomes your life, however bad it is, the familiarity is comforting and it's hard to imagine being without it. The hustle and bustle sounded even noisier that day, knowing I wasn't going to hear it again.

I thought about the first ten years of my sentence and how different they were from the last seven. I had served two different sentences; I had been two different people.

The familiar sound of the key being forced into my cell door brought me back to myself. I knew I was hearing it for the last time. Geoff Cramfield stood there as it opened. He'd aged, his belly had got bigger, but his face was still tough. In many ways, he had felt the rough side of the prison game, too. Whether you're wearing the shirt or the prison tracksuit, you have to deal with the filth and fury of the place. We'd both been there for about the same amount of time. We'd both felt the rough side of The Well. It didn't matter that he wore a uniform and I didn't.

'Come on, lad, it's your day at last,' he was smiling.

I picked up my stuff, looking around to double check that I'd not forgotten anything. I knew I hadn't, but I still did it.

'Don't you want to go home?' he joked.

'Yeah, I'm just looking for . . .' my eyes darted around.

He put his hand on my shoulder, 'David. David. Stop.' I looked him in the eyes. 'It's going to be all right. It's going to be fine.'

We shared a moment.

I slowly walked out of the cell and on to the landing. I looked round, back into the cell in which I had spent so much time. Geoff slammed the door shut.

I walked down the stairs. I breathed in the rancid smell of prison; a smell that I'd known for seventeen years. I heard the shouts, the laughter, the screams, the kicks. I noticed an officer shouting at an inmate, someone else laughing with another. I could see groups of lads huddled together; I could see loners walking aimlessly. Life. Prison life.

The Well would still carry on. The wheel of prison would still turn, even though I was about to get off.

As we walked across the centre, I looked down each wing, the spider legs of the prison, and I watched the madness. The chaos. The craziness. I could sense the years of battles that the wings had experienced.

We walked on to A Wing – my hunting ground for the first half of my prison career. It sent a chill down my spine. I could see a young version of Tommo dealing, while a young lump stood behind him. It doesn't change. Geoff looked at me, noticing what I saw. He smiled; he knew exactly what I was thinking.

He unlocked the gate to lead me to reception. I was metres away from being set free. Metres.

'Wait there, mate.'

He went to the prop cupboard, returning with my clothes. My property. That box hadn't been opened in seventeen years. He took me into one of the rooms where they carry out strip searches. Whenever you enter or leave prison you have to have one.

'Right, lad, I've got to perform a strip search on you . . .' he started to laugh. 'I'm just pulling your leg. Get changed!'

He left the room and let me get on with it. I pulled out my suit. I couldn't believe how much weight I'd lost. It was astonishing. They were the clothes I came in with, so they were the ones I had to leave in. I fixed myself to look as neat as I could.

I walked out of the room and over to the desk where Geoff was waiting with Jack Wise and Jessica Rogers. All three of them looked at me as I walked over. I had a lump in my throat. They'd obviously all made an effort to be on duty on my day of release. As I approached, Geoff handed over some paperwork.

'Sign there, mate. And there's the money you came in with.'

I signed and took the money. Jessica and Jack hadn't said anything. I turned to Jack first.

'You're a great bloke, Jack. Don't change. You make people laugh, they need it in there, ya know.'

'I know, fella. Listen, take care of yourself,' he shook my hand and walked off, bouncing along, as he always did.

'Jessica, I've never met a kinder person in all my life. You're selfless, loving and will do anything to help anyone. You've been there for me more times than I can remember or ever thank you for.'

She had a few tears in her eyes. 'I knew you were a good guy. I knew it, David. I never gave up. Now look at you.'

She kissed me on the cheek and walked off.

'Take care, Jessica,' I said.

She put her hand up to signal. I don't think she was able to speak. The stereotypical image of the screw hating the con is not the full reality. Sure, it can be that way. But when you've spent such a long time with someone, it makes a difference. Relationships will be formed whatever the position you hold in society. That's what makes us human.

'Time to go, mate,' Geoff walked me to the reception gate.

I shook hands with the other screws who were there, all of them wished me well. Geoff put his keys into the door. As the gate opened, I felt butterflies flapping around my stomach. It was a strange, weak sensation. A sadness. I stepped outside on to the yard. The sun crashed on my head. I looked up to the sky. I was just a few metres away. All Geoff had to do was walk me across the yard, through the final gate and I was out. Free.

We slowly crossed the yard, neither of us rushing it. I looked up at the wing to my right. I heard the shouts and screams. The smell. The noise. Flashbacks from the last seventeen years flicked through my mind at a thousand miles an hour. It was my life in slides. I looked up at the wall. The huge, domineering wall that reached the sky. The perimeter of my world. I looked up at it and couldn't believe that years earlier I'd managed to escape over it. It seemed like a lifetime ago. I'd become a different man. And now I was about to move into the next phase of my life.

We finally got to the last gate. We hadn't said a single word to each other as we had walked across the yard. We stopped and he turned to me with his hand held out.

'All the best, son,' he said, in his normal screw voice.

I smiled. I didn't say anything. I didn't take his hand.

'What?' he asked.

There was a moment of silence before I reached out. I put my arms around him. He went rigid in my arms at first. Then I felt him relax. He embraced me back. After all those years, he was like family. He WAS family.

He opened the gate and I stepped outside. I looked round at Geoff one last time. He smiled and shut the gate.

The sun shone brighter than I'd ever seen it. I dropped my bag on the floor. I breathed in through my nostrils. I was overwhelmed by relief. I was overcome by my new beginning. I watched the traffic down on the main road. Smelt the fumes. The dirty fog of ordinary life. I looked back up at the prison wall. I was out. OUT, OUT, OUT, OUT. I walked a few steps, staring up at it as I did so. I started to smile. I finally had a sense of freedom . . .

BRIDGE THE GAP

The waves crashed against the beach as the tide came in. The air was fresh and breezy, with a slight chill to it, but the sun was still out. I walked along the sea wall enjoying the openness and the freedom of the coast.

It was about six months since my release and I'd gone away with Adam and his family for a two-week break at the mobile home he owned by the sea. It'd taken me a while to adjust to the outside world, but I was enjoying every day of my new life. It had been great to get to know Adam's family. Well, it was great to get to know Adam and my father again. The old brotherly banter soon came back. I'd been welcomed with open arms and things were looking good. My worries were beginning to disappear and I was starting to feel like an ordinary civilian again.

Each and every day on holiday, I'd take a long walk or jog beside the sea wall. I loved the feeling it gave me, being so close to the ocean. The elements are a thing of beauty to most people, but after my prison sentence they became even more than just that to me.

I'd run for four or five miles. I was heading back to the campsite and was walking the last half mile or so, just looking out to sea and thinking. I found it calming and I knew that it would be somewhere near the coast and close to nature that I would settle down.

I'd offered to collect fish and chips for everyone on my way back. As I got closer to the campsite, I could hear a really bad version of my 'My Way' being sung. The outdoor karaoke was in full swing.

I walked down the stairs from the sea wall to the parade of pubs, cafés and chip shops. It was packed with hoards of people drinking beer, kids running around and the wannabe pop stars belting out tunes on the karaoke. The smell of fried food, beer and sun cream was a beautiful thing. A working-class paradise. Life in all its glory. I smiled to myself as I looked at it all.

I walked through the groups of people, dodging the drunks and smiling at the ladies. I got closer to the chip shop and was about to step in, when I saw a sweet little girl standing next to it, crying her eyes out. She couldn't have been any more than six or seven. I stopped and looked around to see who she was with. The world rushed all around her, no one took any notice whatsoever. She was obviously lost. I walked over and knelt down to speak to her.

'Is everything OK?' I asked.

'I . . . I . . . I can't find . . . I . . . I . . .' she was struggling to get her words out through the tears.

'You with your mum and dad?' I asked her.

'Yes, I . . . I . . . can't find them.'

'OK, don't worry. You see that over there?' I pointed to the karaoke stage just a few feet away. 'If you walk over there, I'll go with you and we'll ask the man to call your mum and dad over to the microphone.'

She started to walk with me. We'd only taken a few steps when she sprinted off through the crowd. I watched her run about fifteen metres or so, then jump up at a nervous-looking man. A middle-aged guy with a well-fed stomach, thick grey hair and glasses. He picked the little girl up and I could see the relief washing over him. I stopped and looked, smiling at them both. The man turned round, so I could see the whole of his face. Memories came flooding back. Everything. Playing football, watching videos, climbing trees. Then, the more sinister activities – the drugs, the violence, the intimidation. And finally my prison sentence. All of the past I had shared with Donnie.

And there he was, only a few metres away from me. I'd not seen him since the day I left that lock up. The day I was arrested. And I was never supposed to see him again. But, by chance, there he stood, just a few steps away. My chest felt tight. I was shaky and nervous. He still hadn't seen me. The memories. How they came back to me. He looked so different that I had hardly recognised him. His weight gain, his clothes, his age. Perhaps not as much as I had changed, though. Scars still covered my face and body from Casey's attack, but I was fitter and healthier than I'd ever been before. Nearly twenty years and a whole lifetime had passed. A time of new memories, changes to both of us, physically and mentally. We'd changed. I had definitely changed.

As Donnie held the little girl, she said something to him and pointed over to me. Donnie looked round and glanced my way. He raised his hand to thank me for the help I'd given her. I smiled nervously and waved back.

I didn't feel anger; I didn't feel anything other than sadness. He had done what he needed to do back then. He had a family and wanted to give them a life; protect them from everything. Protect them from me. I could say that I had forgiven him for turning me in. But there was nothing to forgive. He took the path that was laid down for him. It wasn't a choice, but a necessity. I felt sad that we'd spent so many years as friends, spent so much time together in the early days, and now it was all different. It was a shame that we couldn't have remained friends and been close after all those years.

We'd both come along way. We both had more rewarding

lives now. Was the little girl his daughter? Or maybe his granddaughter? Whoever she was, Donnie looked like a man who had a life worth living, as did I.

He started to walk off and I watched him go, carrying the little girl. As he got a few more metres away, he stopped and looked back at me. Our eyes met and he smiled in recognition. He knew.

He turned around again and continued on his way. I've never seen him since . . .

A BUS COULD RUN
YOU OVER

I'm fifty-one years old and I've been out of prison for three years. Looking back, I've lived a complex life, full of challenges. I did some atrocious things that many would say are unforgivable. Perhaps they're right. But I will make one thing clear, I regret every last one of them. I don't say that because it's the right thing to say. I always say what I feel.

I believe karma has dealt with me. Do I think I've been fully tried for all my wrongs? I don't know. What I've come to learn is that doing good will help you receive good. That might not sound revolutionary but, if it isn't, why don't more people actually practise it?

It took a life of crime, violence and drug abuse for me to realise the very simple facts of life. I live life to the full now and always thank God for the pleasure of being able to do so. I do unto others as they do to me. When you step back and see what living is all about – I mean really see what it's about – being happy and enjoying this prize is not so difficult.

Finding faith helped me realise that. Having a relationship with God and going through the mental and physical tortures that I went through made me see life from a whole other angle.

Perhaps I did get served my just deserts in prison. Did prison work for me? I don't believe it did. Part of what happened was due to my past wrongs, but that doesn't excuse some of the treatment I had when I was ill. And ill is what I was. Spiritually and mentally. They couldn't have helped me with the former, but the latter they most certainly could have. Maybe if they had, my realisation would have come sooner? I'm not blaming them for all my savage violence. But I do believe that if I had been helped a little more, then there may have been a few more people saved from my fist. I was a sick man.

I now live a very simple life on the Essex/Suffolk border. I go for long walks. I enjoy nature. I live in a small cottage. The scenic area and the beautiful world around me remind me to respect and thank the Creator for helping me attain my new and wonderful life.

I've not yet met someone to share my days with. That is something I'm longing for; a partner, a wife. I've no doubt when the time is right, I will meet her.

I see my family as often as I can, and I have a wonderful relationship with all of them.

I learned how to teach music, which is how I now earn a living. I also teach yoga and meditation. I don't hide my past from anyone – it's part of who I am today. But I use it as an example of how you can change. I've helped many of my clients through that demonstration.

There's a common saying that you should never judge a book by its cover. It's true, it's not the cover you should take notice of, but the words that are written underneath.

God bless . . .

More Non-fiction from Headline Review

SCREWED

RONNIE THOMPSON

'Honest, brutal, gripping' Garry Bushell

DRUGS. VIOLENCE. CORRUPTION.

And that's just the screws.

My name is Ronnie Thompson. Being a Prison Officer
for Her Majesty's Prison Service was something I used
to be proud of. I soon realised the truth of what it's
like working as a screw – the danger, pressures, duties,
life-wrecking conditions – a fucking headache.

Ronnie Thompson tells it like it is. For the first time
ever, a Prison Officer reveals what really goes
on behind bars.

He exposes the underworld of bent screws, the drugs
they traffic, the firms they work for and what they get
paid for their sins. He talks about the times when force
is necessary and used, and when it is unnecessary
but still used.

Ultimately, he shows that being a good screw doesn't
always mean sticking to the rules . . .

NON-FICTION / Memoir 978 0 7553 1666 3